The Power of the Earth

Dr. CV. White

The Power of the Earth
Dr. Cynthia V. White

All rights reserved. No part of this book may be reproduced or transmitted in any form or by any means, electronic or mechanical including photocopying, recording, or by any information storage or retrieval system, without written permission from the author.

Unless otherwise quoted all word definitions Greek and Hebrew and scripture quotations are from the King James Version of the Bible as recorded in the Blue Letter Bible: Retrieved from http://www.blueletterbible.org. All other scripture quotations from the amplified Bible were retrieved from the biblegateway.com by the Lockman Foundation or International Standard Bible Encyclopedia, Electronic Database, Copyright © 1995-1996, 2003 by Biblesoft, Inc., All rights reserved, The New Unger's Bible Dictionary - Originally published by Moody Press of Chicago, Illinois, Copyright © 1988. Research definitions from Wikipedia, the free encyclopedia

ISBN-13: 978-1-934326-06-0
ISBN-10: 1-934326-06-2

Copyright © 2015 by Dr CV. White

Published by:
Dr. CV. White formerly Fruit That Remain Publishing
150 Post Office Road Waldorf, Maryland 20604
Email: drcvwhite@gmail.com

Printed in the United States of America

DEDICATION

This book is dedicated my biological father, Rev. Lee Andrew Townes Sr., who helped me to mature naturally and spiritually. He is the seed from which I came. My father was an inspiration to me as my father and as my pastor for many years. He started to preach when he was eight years old and continued for seventy-two years. For fifty of those years he pastored churches, and during that time he was instrumental in the spiritual growth of many aspiring pastors and clergy. Also, I thank Bishop Rodney S. Walker, I, my spiritual father, who has been instrumental in my spiritual growth. Bishop Walker, I appreciate your support while I was attending school, working, and preparing for ministry. You have been and still are a great blessing to me! Every step of the way you encouraged me to continue with my writing projects. I am appreciative of all of your efforts to assist me in this project and in other areas of my life. I also appreciate God for giving me such a wonderful spiritual father in you! You are a special gift from God and I will always cherish everything that you have poured into me all of these years.

I want to thank my Mother Cynthia Ollie Mary Townes Turner for giving birth to me and helping me in every way she possible could. I want to thank my Children, Myrna White, Gregory T. White Jr. and Lance White, Larry White, Laura White and Denise, and all of their children and the generations that follow to let them know how much I appreciate them and God for making it possible for all of them to be a part of me.

APPRECIATION

I would like to take this opportunity to thank Fruit That Remain Publishing LLC, Bishop Rodney S. Walker, I., Cynthia Anglin, Michelle Browning, Paulette Walker, Lisa Burgess and Divine Purpose Publishing for their support and assistance in the preparation of this book for publication.

I appreciate your willingness to meet the challenges necessary to complete the final preparation for printing and distribution. Your ideas and suggestions contributed immensely to the success of this project. It was so good to have you as part of the team. I am confident that good things will come from our joint efforts. Thank you, again, for a job well done!

Table of Contents

Chapter 1- What is the Earth?..7

Chapter 2- Man's Ability to Grow Spiritual Things...............11

Chapter 3- God Has Given Earth the Power to Bring Forth.........14

Chapter 4- Spiritual Production.................................... 20

Chapter 5- Birthing Spiritual Things with God.................... 35

Chapter 6- Growing Your Seed 43

Chapter 7- Rejoice and Be Glad....................................49

Chapter 8- The Husbandman 55

Chapter 9- Holy Spirit Our Enabler and Our Helper.............62

Chapter 10- The Mystery of the Earthen Vessel 74

Chapter 11- Chosen Vessels..89

The Power of the Earth

Chapter 1 - What is the Earth?

What is the earth and how is it connected with man. God has prepared it for man but how is it connected? God has made it beautiful to look at and wonderful to live in but how is it connected to us? God has provided everything that we need to live comfortably here on earth but how is it connected with us? God has prepared everything that the earth needs to function but how does that impact us? There is power in the earth that God has put there and that same power is in us.

Before we get started we must get a clear definition of the word earth. The first mention of the word earth is in ***Gen 1:1 In the beginning God created the heaven and the earth.*** Notice that the word earth is mentioned in the very first verse, which means it has significant value and position in the organization of things. The Hebrew word for earth is 'erets and it means land, earth, whole earth (as opposed to a part), earth (as opposed to heaven), earth (inhabitants), land, country, territory, district, region, tribal territory, piece of ground, land of Canaan, Israel, inhabitants of land, Sheol, land without return, (under) world, city (state) ground, surface of the earth, ground, soil, (in phrases) people of the land, space or distance of country (in measurements of distance) level or plain country, land of the living, end(s) of the earth, (almost wholly late in usage) lands, countries, often in contrast to Canaan.

Now this is interesting because God created the heaven and the earth, we are focusing on the earth. The earth was created with 'soil' that is also called earth and was given all it needed in order for it to grow things. The whole earth has some land masses that cannot grow things, and that is also called earth. The inhabitants of the earth are also called earth. This is amazing because they are all connected in that they are all a part of the whole. The inhabitants consists of animals, birds, reptiles, etc. and man. However man has a more specialized relationship with a particular part of the earth and that is the soil. We see that in Gen 2:7:

Gen 2:7 <u>And the LORD God formed man of the dust of the ground</u>, and breathed into his nostrils the breath of life; and man became a living soul.

In this verse the word dust in Hebrew is `aphar which is a masculine noun which means dry earth, dust, powder, ashes, earth, ground, mortar, rubbish, dry or loose earth, debris, ore and according to the Free Online

Dictionary soil is defined as the following things: The top layer of the earth's surface, consisting of rock and mineral particles, mixed with organic matter, 2. A particular kind of earth or ground: sandy soil, 3.

Country; land: native soil, 4. The agricultural life: a man of the soil and 5. a place or condition favorable to growth; a breeding ground.

The soil is the loose dust top layer of the earth, therefore we understand that God used the same loose soil to form man; in addition Gen. 2:7 also says that God formed man of the dust of the ground. The definition of ground in this verse comes from the Hebrew word 'adamah which is a feminine noun which means ground, land ground (as general, tilled, yielding sustenance) piece of ground, a specific plot of land, earth substance (for building or constructing), ground as earth's visible surface, land, territory, country, whole inhabited earth. This adamah is the substance that grows things. God formed man of the dust of the adamah and God called him Adam. We know that God had deposited substances in the earth that grows plants, trees, vines etc. and now Adam and the adamah can both grow things.

The secular dictionaries define earth very similar to the Hebrew definition; it defines earth as the whole earth, the inhabitants and the dry land and ground. One dictionary definition is found in The Dicitonary.com - earth is 1.(often initial capital letter) the planet third in order from the sun, having an equatorial diameter of 7926 miles (12,755 km) and a polar diameter of 7900 miles (12,714 km), a mean distance from the sun of 92.9 million miles (149.6 million km), and a period of revolution of 365.26 days, and having one satellite. 2. the inhabitants of this planet, especially the human inhabitants: The whole earth rejoiced. 3. this planet as the habitation of humans, often in contrast to heaven and hell: to create a hell on earth. 4. the surface of this planet: to fall to earth. 5. the solid matter of this planet; dry land; ground.

God's final work with forming man was to blow the breath of life into him and he became a living soul. Remember in **Gen 2:7: *And the LORD God formed man of the dust of the ground, and breathed into his nostrils the breath of life; and man became a living soul.***

Adamah is not a living soul but it can grow things (plants, flowers, trees etc.), Adam is a living soul, he has the same power to grow things because he was formed from that growing substance adamah, but he cannot in his body (earth) grow plants, trees etc. If not plants and trees, what is it that grows in Adam? Man (Adam-Mankind) grows spiritual things.

Chapter 2 – Man's Ability to Grow Spiritual Things

God has prepared a natural environment for us to connect to that will give us a picture and an understanding of spiritual things and how to connect with and understand spiritual things.

Jesus explained this mystery in Mark chapter 4 when He talked about the seed and the sower. Jesus used a natural happening to explain a spiritual truth. But let us examine the earth and how it relates to us first.

We belong to God and He has positioned us to prosper in everything we do because He has given us the ability to grow things without having to add or take away from the process. Since it is possible for us to grow things we can prosper in what God desires just by planting the right seed and also whose report we believe. If we believe the report of the Lord and follow after Him we will find ourselves growing in grace. We do get to choose what we want to grow, however we have nothing to do with the substance that causes us to grow.

Let's start with Gen. 1:10:

Gen. 1:10 And God called the dry [land] Earth; and the gathering together of the waters called the Seas: and God saw that [it was] good.

The Hebrew definition of earth in this passage is 'egrets feminine noun –from root word to be firm, it is land, earth, earth (inhabitants), and inhabitants of land. This is the same word found in Gen. 1:1 and this same definition applies to the inhabitants of the earth in:

Gen. 11:1 And the whole <u>earth</u> was of one language, and of one speech. KJV

The Hebrew definition of earth on one hand is the land and on the other it is the earth's inhabitants. God called the land earth – only the land is earth – so all of the land inhabitants were of one language and one speech. God allowed the earth to reproduce the things He put in the earth. The seed (natural and spiritual) needs the earth to reproduce. The seed cannot reproduce by itself. It needs the earth to complete the process. It was the earth that brought forth the grass and the trees etc. We see that in:

Gen. 1:11-12. And God said, Let the earth bring forth grass, the herb yielding seed, [and] the fruit tree yielding fruit after his kind, whose seed [is] in itself, upon the earth: and it was so. ¹² And the earth brought forth grass, [and] herb yielding seed after his kind, and the tree yielding fruit, whose seed [was] in itself, after his kind: and God saw that [it was] good. KJV

Notice the earth was given the command to bring forth and it brought forth. The Hebrew for brought forth is "yatsa" it is a verb and it means to go out, come out, exit, go forth, cause to go or come out, bring out, lead out.

Notice in verse 11 *God commanded the earth to bring forth and the earth brought out of the ground the seed of grass, yielding seed of its own kind, grass, [and] herb yielding seed after his kind, and the tree yielding fruit, whose seed [was] in itself, after his kind: and God saw that [it was] good. KJV.* God prepared the earth to do this and this ability to grow things is all in the ground, not in the seed.

So it is with us. We are spiritual ground and we are commanded to bring forth and give birth to spiritual things. Bring forth occurs 499 times in 403 verses in the Hebrew, there we see the law of most mentioned going into play. God is serious about us bringing forth. When He created the earth He put the substance in it to bring forth.

Chapter 3 - God Has Given Earth Power to Bring Forth

When God spoke to the serpent that represents Satan in:

Genesis 3:15 And I will put enmity between thee and the woman, and between thy seed and her seed; it shall bruise thy head, and thou shalt bruise his heel KJV.

He was not just speaking to him about Adam, the man with the womb (woman), as Adam had called her but also to His bride, the body of Christ. The body of Christ is the bride of Christ and therefore His woman. When John the Baptist was asked of the people if he were the Christ he said no, he was only a friend of the bridegroom and then explained to them the bride belonged to the bridegroom in:

John 3:28-29 Ye yourselves bear me witness, that I said, I am not the Christ, but that I am sent before him, [29] He that hath the bride is the bridegroom: but the friend of the bridegroom, which standeth and heareth him, rejoiceth greatly because of the bridegroom's voice: this my joy therefore is fulfilled.

Now this is interesting because Jesus likened His followers

as a woman giving birth when He was telling them of His leaving them, we find that in:

John 16:19-23 Now Jesus knew that they were desirous to ask him, and said unto them, Do ye enquire among yourselves of that I said, A little while, and ye shall not see me: and again, a little while, and ye shall see me? 20 Verily, verily, I say unto you, That ye shall weep and lament, but the world shall rejoice: and ye shall be sorrowful, but your sorrow shall be turned into joy. 21 A woman when she is in travail hath sorrow, because her hour is come: but as soon as she is delivered of the child, she remembereth no more the anguish, for joy that a man is born into the world. 22 And ye now therefore have sorrow: but I will see you again, and your heart shall rejoice, and your joy no man taketh from you. 23 And in that day ye shall ask me nothing. Verily, verily, I say unto you, Whatsoever ye shall ask the Father in my name, he will give it you.

We see from this that Jesus does consider believers as His Bride; this is also addressed in Jeremiah and Isaiah. One particular instance in Isaiah can be found in:

Isaiah 61:10-11 I will greatly rejoice in the LORD, my soul shall be joyful in my God; for he hath clothed me with the garments of salvation, he hath covered me with the robe of righteousness, as a bridegroom decketh himself with ornaments, and as a bride adorneth herself with her jewels.

And here in verse 11 Isaiah mentions bringing forth:

¹¹ For as the earth bringeth forth her bud, and as the garden causeth the things that are sown in it to spring forth; so the Lord GOD will cause righteousness and praise to spring forth before all the nations.

Now when God spoke to the woman in Genesis we see that God has positioned her to bring forth in Gen 3:16 Unto the woman **(the body of Christ)** he said, I will greatly multiply thy sorrow and thy conception; in sorrow thou shalt bring forth children (God is speaking to the earth and commanding it to bring forth, just as He did the ground in Genesis 1:11-12) the word children in the Hebrew is 'ben' meaning son, grandson, child, member of a group a) son, male child b) grandson c) children (pl. - male and female) d) youth, young men (pl.) e) young (of animals) f) sons (as characterization, i.e. sons of injustice [for unrighteous men] or sons of God [for angels] g) people (of a nation) (pl.) h) of lifeless things, i.e. sparks, stars, arrows (fig.) i) a member of a guild, order, class. The children of God give birth to natural children but also spiritual children.

God continues talking to His woman and says and thy desire [shall be] to thy husband **(Jesus Christ)** and he shall rule over thee. God was not talking about just Eve here because He called her – "Adam". Adam called her Eve after God had spoken to both of them after their disobedience. God is talking about His woman, the church (His Bride).

We see that in the passage before when He spoke to the Serpent (resenting the Devil) about his fate in Gen 3:15 – God said "And I will put enmity which is the Hebrew word 'eybah meaning hatred - between thee and the woman, between thy seed (the seed of Satan) and her seed (Jesus Christ); it shall bruise – the Hebrew word for bruise is shuwph meaning to bruise, crush, gape upon, desire, seize, strike out a) (Qal) to fall upon, break thy head. The Hebrew for head here is ro'sh meaning head, top, summit, upper part, chief, total, sum, height, front, beginning a) head (of man, animals) b) top, tip (of mountain) c) height (of stars) d) chief, head (of man, city, nation, place, family, priest) e) head, front, beginning f) chief, choicest, best g) head, division, company, band h) sum and thou shalt bruise his heel and the Hebrew for heel is `aqeb meaning heel, rear, footprint, hinder part, hoof, rear of a troop, footstep a) heel b) mark of heel, footprint c) hinder part, rear. So you see God was talking about the work of Christ and what that work would empower us as His woman to do.

If women understood this, many of them would no longer be offended by people who belittle women, label them as second class and communicate the idea that God has made women less than men in every aspect of human life. Think about it, the world hates the church (God's woman), Christians are the only ones that cannot publicly display Christ in non-Christian environments without some kind of objection or protest. That I believe is the main reason women go through this kind of aggravation. It is not personal for females. It is just that females are women in the natural and they demonstrate in the natural what happens in the spirit. Men are also God's woman therefore, they can glean from this persecution of women in the natural as what to expect in the spirit. God wants us to bring forth the things of God and make the earth look like heaven, women in the natural can understand bringing forth more so than men, however men can understand being the seed more so than women. Both are needed to complete the growing process. The earth needs the seed and the seed needs the earth. The earth has the God given power to bring forth. Using the power to bring forth is very important, it is something that we are expected to do and the more we bring forth the more of the same is required. In the natural the woman becomes the earth that receives the seed from the man. The seed cannot reproduce without the assistance of the earth.

Jesus explains this better in:

John 15:2 Every branch in me that beareth not fruit he taketh away: and every [branch] that beareth fruit, he purgeth it, that it may bring forth more fruit.

We see here that God wants us to bring forth fruit and Jesus is explaining that in order to bring forth what God wants us to, we have to be connected with Jesus Christ:

John 15:16 Ye have not chosen me, but I have chosen you, and ordained you, that ye should go and bring forth fruit, and [that] your fruit should remain: that whatsoever ye shall ask of the Father in my name, he may give it you.

We are chosen and ordained to bring forth fruit and it is possible to do this because the power is in the earth provided by God through Jesus Christ.

Now we can consider in earnest our responsibility to bring forth as the bride of Christ collectively and individually, this is mentioned in:

Rom 7:4 Wherefore, my brethren, ye also are become dead to the law by the body of Christ; that ye should be married to another, [even] to him who is raised from the dead, that we should bring forth fruit unto God.

Notice what Jesus commanded us to do in the New Testament concerning bringing forth. We see that in the three passages listed here but there are many more that clarify our bringing forth. We can produce already. We are not waiting for God to empower us to produce. We are the ground that produces spiritual things.

Chapter 4 - Spiritual Production

When God spoke to the earth in the Old Testament, the earth obeyed God. Now as God has prepared us with the substance the earth has, He expects us to speak to the earth also using the ministry of Holy Spirit to help us accomplish what He has commanded us to do. So now Jesus is saying bring forth fruit and His expectation of us matches God ability to do anything, therefore everything is possible by just asking God for it in the name of Jesus. We have God in us, Holy Spirit and that means that our earth (ground) is power packed with ability to grow things.

Bring Forth in the Greek is poieō occurs 602 times in 519 verses and it mean to make: a) with the names of things made, to produce, construct, form, fashion, etc. b) to be the authors of, the cause c) to make ready, to prepare d) to produce, bear, shoot forth e) to acquire, to provide a thing for one's self f) to make a thing out of something g) to (make i.e.) render one anything 1) to (make i.e.) constitute or appoint one anything, to appoint or ordain one that 2) to (make i.e.) declare one anything h) to put one forth, to lead him out i) to make one do something 1) cause one to and also to perform: to a promise. Understanding this definition along with the presence of Holy Spirit means that nothing is impossible for us to bring forth.

God also allowed the earth to reproduce living animals (all of the living creatures, insects, snakes, cattle, all living things) and they reproduce after their own kind but they needed the earth to start the process. We see that in Gen 1:24-25:

Gen 1:24-25 And God said, Let the earth bring forth the living creature after his kind, cattle, and creeping thing, and beast of the earth after his kind: and it was so. 25 And God made the beast of the earth after his kind, and cattle after their kind, and every thing that creepeth upon the earth after his kind: and God saw that [it was] good.

Then God used the same earth to form man and we see that in Gen 2:7, however God breathed the breath of life into man and man became a living soul, thus God created man in His image and as His likeness.

Gen 2:7 And the LORD God formed man [of] the dust of the ground, and breathed into his nostrils the breath of life; and man became a living soul.

Now we can see a portion of the mind of God concerning the earth, but God never intended for the earth to produce without an ingredient that would wake up the growing power that God has put in it to cause things to grow.

The earth needs something to ignite it and cause what is in it to produce and that is water, light (heat) and air. So in order for things to grow they need the earth and the earth needs the help of water, light and air. Plants need good soil that contains the minerals plants need for nutrients. These minerals dissolve into the water in the ground. The water is taken in by the roots. The plants need sunlight that is absorbed through the plant's leaves and also air that is also taken in through the leaves.

God provided all of these things; let us take a look at the light first in Gen 1:14-18:

Gen 1:14 And God said, Let there be lights in the firmament of the heaven to divide the day from the night; and let them be for signs, and for seasons, and for days, and years: Gen 1:15 And let them be for lights in the firmament of the heaven to give light upon the earth: and it was so.

So you see from this passage that God provided the light for plants that are planted in the earth. They need the light as a part of their growth process.

Gen 1:16 And God made two great lights; the greater light to rule the day, and the lesser light to rule the night: [he made] the stars also. Gen 1:17 And God set them in the firmament of the heaven to give light upon the earth, Gen 1:18 And to rule over the day and over the night, and to divide the light from the darkness: and God saw that [it was] good.

The next ingredient that plants need to grow is water and we can see that God provided the water in:

Gen 1:10 And God called the dry [land] Earth; and the gathering together of the waters called the Seas: and God saw that [it was] good.

God also used water to bring fourth some things in:

Gen 1:20-22. And God said, Let the waters bring forth abundantly the moving creature that hath life, and fowl [that] may fly above the earth in the open firmament of heaven. [21] And God created great whales, and every living creature that moveth, which the waters brought forth abundantly, after their kind, and every winged fowl after his kind: and God saw that [it was] good. [22] And God blessed them, saying, Be fruitful, and multiply, and fill the waters in the seas, and let fowl multiply in the earth.

God also watered the earth with water. Take a look at:

Gen. 2:5-6 And every plant of the field before it was in the earth, and every herb of the field before it grew: for the LORD God had not caused it to rain upon the earth, and [there was] not a man to till the ground. Gen 2:6 But there went up a mist from the earth, and watered the whole face of the ground.

We see here where God caused the earth of be watered and He watered the whole face of the ground. So we know that the ground needs water. In addition, the ground needed to be tilled or plowed but there was not a man to do that. Remember this because we will talk about the importance of tilling the ground later.

The earth produces for natural things like the plants with the help of light and water, we as believers produce spiritual things with the help of light (Jesus Christ) – We see that Jesus is the light in:

John 1:1-5 In the beginning was the Word, and the Word was with God, and the Word was God. ² The same was in the beginning with God. ³ All things were made by him; and without him was not any thing made that was made. ⁴ <u>In him was life; and the life was the light of men.</u> ⁵ <u>And the light shineth in darkness; and the darkness comprehended it not.</u>

Now, mankind has the light that is needed for them to grow things, the life source comes from Christ and that life becomes the light of men. We are made of what is in the earth that grows things, but we need to have the light as a part of our growth process. The light we need is in the person of Jesus Christ, therefore we must have Jesus in order to get the light for ourselves or to be the light to help someone else to grow things. Jesus said that He was that light while He was in the world and now that He is gone we are the light. We see that in:

John 9:5 As long as I am in the world, I am the light of the world. And then we see that we are the light in *Mat 5:14 Ye are the light of the world. A city that is set on an hill cannot be hid* and also in *John 8:12, Then spake Jesus again unto them, saying, I am the light of the world: he that followeth me shall not walk in darkness, but shall have the light of life.*

We must consider that God is the origin of light and He called the light forth in:

Gen 1:3 KJV (And God said, Let there be light: and there was light.)

Before He gave it to the sun, moon or the stars and while they all shine in the natural, the light that God has given us comes directly from Him.

As we take a look at light remember that things in the spirit are more real than things in the natural. God wanted us to understand spiritually how this all works concerning the power of growing things. We have already talked about how the sun gives the light that is needed for the growth of plants etc. but the earth has the ability to bring forth the seed of the plants. The spiritual light that the earth in John 9:5 phōs, this is the Greek for the word light, it means the light emitted by a lamp, a heavenly light such as surrounds angels when they appear on earth, anything emitting light, a star, fire because it is light and sheds light, a lamp or torch, light, i.e brightness of a lamp, metaph.

God is light and because light has an extremely delicate, subtle, pure, and brilliant quality of truth its knowledge together with the spiritual purity associated with it is exposed in the view of all. It cannot be hidden. It is displayed, openly, publicly, by reason and mind, the power of understanding especially moral and spiritual truth. Putting this in simple terms nothing is hidden in the light. Anything that the light shines on or that is in the light will be seen. It will be seen openly, publicly with brilliance and in truth. It will expose the moral and spiritual truth with the power needed to understand either one.

This is truly powerful because we really have to understand the function of the sun light in order to understand the light of God. Some things cannot be seen at night in the darkness, but when the sun light appears everything can be seen. God is light; this is one of the characteristics of God. This lets us know that anytime we want to hide something that behavior is not God operating in our lives because God is light. For example, when are talking about people's personal business and (gossip) we are operating in darkness. Most of the time the folks that are doing that do not want it known that they are putting someone's business out there for public knowledge.

Have you ever notice how we always want to hide things that are sinful? I can remember so many things that I was doing that I did not want anybody to know especially those things that I knew were wrong. I wanted those things to be kept in the dark. You cannot grow things of life in the dark but you can experience death in darkness. Plants need the light to grow and so do we.

Just think about it, we don't want people to know what we said or did when we knew that it was wrong. One of the first things that people will tell people that they are about to abuse or misuse is "Don't tell anybody" and that is an effort to keep the light from shinning on it and exposing it in truth. They want that deed or event kept in the dark.

When we learn to keep the personal business of other people confidential we are operating in the light of God.

That is not hiding things from people. That is not giving people information that they are not authorized to have. When God opens a person's file to you and gives you information that they did not share or when God sends a person to you to share information it is because you can help them. That information is now in the light but only to those authorized to have the information.

We need the light of God to grow things, it is not easy to admit when you are hungry for the wrong things and that we want to keep them in the dark so that no one will know, but God wants to grow things, naturally and spiritually and they both require light. Sometimes God will tell us individually or corporately that we need to let go of some things and release them to Him so that we can be free of that particular issue before the light comes. God wants to help us get rid of things privately before they come to the light. We are working on our soul's salvation from all of those bad habits that we learned before we were saved and we are removing them one by one or even more if possible depending on the individual.

Once we are free of any of those things and we have the revelation of what the word of God says about that situation we can begin to walk in that light. We can then add that to the light we are already walking in and now our span of light covers more territory.

Things do grow in the dark, but they are not of God. Darkness is not found in God. God does give us an earthly natural representation of that so we can know that it is possible to grow things for Satan but it must be done in the dark. The nature of Satan is to operate in darkness but God has delivered us from that. We see that in:

Col 1:13 Who hath delivered us from the power of darkness, and hath translated us into the kingdom of his dear Son who provides our spiritual light.

The example that I remember of things that grow in the dark is a Poinsettia plant, to force a Poinsettia into a bloom by Christmas, you need to provide 12 hours of total darkness every day, beginning in late September or early October. It must be in total darkness, no light can hit it at all if you are to get what appears to be a beautiful flower blooming by Christmas. Now the blooms are not blooms at all but modified leaves, so if you do not look closely you may be fooled into thinking that it is a flower blooming. This is a natural example of how you can think you are bringing something forth for God and it is actually for Satan. If you have to hide it, it is not God.

The Poinsettia is a beautiful display of red leaves not flowers. People say all the time that the red leaves are red flowers but they are not they are leaves. I am not saying that it is bad, everything that God made is good, even though everything that God created is good it is possible to use it to understand what is not good. I love poinsettias and I get some every year, but I do understand that God brought me out of darkness into His marvelous light because I had lots of hidden things. I was not only hiding my issues, I was hiding myself. I want fragrant flowers that require light not weeds with red leaves that require darkness.

Paul explains what some hidden things are in:

2 Cr 4:2-4 But have renounced the hidden things of dishonesty, not walking in craftiness, nor handling the word of God deceitfully; but by manifestation of the truth commending ourselves to every man's conscience in the sight of God. 3 But if our gospel be hid, it is hid to them that are lost: 4 In whom the god of this world hath blinded the minds of them which believe not, lest the light of the glorious gospel of Christ, who is the image of God, should shine unto them. You see how God wants us to use the light to help us bring forth the things of God. We need the light to help us grow. We need to understand how important it is to stay in the light because when we do that we grow in grace. Peter explains that in:

2 Pe 3:18 But grow in grace, and in the knowledge of our Lord and Saviour Jesus Christ. To him be glory both now and forever. Amen.

Now let's talk about water and how we need it to grow things. Jesus also explained the function of water in us. We need living water to help us produce spiritual things. God gave us water as a part of what makes things grow and live, some life form need very little water, others can survive a long time without it but so far water is essential for all known life forms on earth. But to make things simple, if you have ever had a potted plant this is one of the greatest lessons of understanding water. If you do not water it the plant will die, it has everything else that it needs, soil (earth), nutrients including fertilizer and light but if you for- get to add water on a regular basis it will die, and what is also interesting is that sometimes the plant will seem to be almost dead and when you add water it comes to life again. Water can be in three different forms, solid, liquid and gas and God mentions all three of them in the Bible. What we can surmise from this is that water is needed in some form for every form of life naturally and spiritually.

God gave Isaiah some valuable insight about water and its importance in our lives in:

Isaiah 55:10 For as the rain cometh down, and the snow from heaven, and returneth not thither, but watereth the earth, and maketh it bring forth and bud, that it may give seed to the sower, and bread to the eater: KJV

We see from this passage that water makes the earth bring forth and bud. This is an indication that we as earth need water. The water we need for life comes from Jesus Christ. Jesus told the woman at the well that living water was a gift from God just for the asking:

John 4:10 Jesus answered and said unto her, If thou knewest the gift of God, and who it is that saith to thee, Give me to drink; thou wouldest have asked of him, and he would have given thee living water KJV

God called Himself the fountain of living waters in:

Jer 2:13 For my people have committed two evils; they have forsaken me the fountain of living waters, [and] hewed them out cisterns, broken cisterns, that can hold no water.

And how important it is to be able to hold the living waters, in fact it is evil to forsake the living water and to position yourself not to be able to receive and carry the living waters because we need the living waters of God in order to bring forth and bud spiritual things.

In addition, we that believe in Him shall also produce water, according to:

John 4:14 But whosoever drinketh of the water that I shall give him shall never thirst; but the water that I shall give him shall be in him a well of water springing up into everlasting life. John 7:38 He that believeth on me, as the scripture hath said, out of his belly shall flow rivers of living water.

Holy Spirit is not water but He brings us water. For believers that spiritual water comes from our precious Holy Spirit. When we allow the ministry of Holy Spirit to be a vital part of our lives and invite Him in to speak, He will say what He knows that God wants to say and not what we want to say. When Holy Spirit speaks whatever He speaks to, whoever He speaks to, or whoever He speaks of will receive the living waters and begin to come forth because His living waters will make us (the earth) bring forth.

Remember we said earlier that plants and trees etc. need soil, air, light, and space to grow and we need these things also to grow spiritual things. We are the ground (soil) and the space; we covered the light and the water, now we need to cover the air (wind) – The ministry of Holy Spirit also provides the air that we need to help us produce spiritual things. Holy Spirit is symbolic of water and air (wind). We have already mentioned water let us take a look at air (wind) in the following passages:

John 3:8 The wind bloweth where it listeth, and thou hearest the sound thereof, but canst not tell whence it cometh, and whither it goeth: so is every one that is born of the Spirit. And in Act 2:2 And suddenly there came a sound from heaven as of a rushing mighty wind, and it filled all the house where they were sitting.

Notice that John said Holy Spirit came as of a mighty rushing wind. He was not wind but He came as wind. The Holy Spirit is God and He knows all things and because He knows all things we know all things because we are smeared with Him and He is also in us. This is confirmed in:

1 John 2:20 But ye have an unction from the Holy One, and ye know all things KJV.

Unction in this verse is the Greek word *chrisma* which means anything smeared on, unguent, ointment, usually prepared by the Hebrews from oil and aromatic herbs. Anointing was the inaugural ceremony for priests and we know that we are a royal priesthood; therefore all we have to do is submit to the ministry of Holy Spirit and allow Him to say what He wants to say through us. Have you ever watched the leaves blow in the wind? You cannot tell where it came from or where it is going and because we can't tell we need Holy Spirit to help us because He knows what is going on all the time. You might be thinking well we can just ask God, but we don't even know what to ask God sometimes and that is another reason the ministry of the Holy Spirit is so important. He prays for us when we don't know what to pray for and that is recorded in:

Rom 8:26 Likewise the Spirit also helpeth our infirmities: for we know not what we should pray for as we ought: but the Spirit itself maketh intercession for us with groanings which cannot be uttered. KJV

You may be saying how can we bring forth if we have no examples? John gives us the answer in:

John 14:26 But the Comforter, [which is] the Holy Ghost, whom the Father will send in my name, he shall teach you all things, and bring all things to your remembrance, whatsoever I have said unto you. - John 14:26 KJV,

We must study the word of God, remember Jesus is the word of God and we do that because we are the sons of God. As we study the word of God, Holy Spirit will teach us and give us revelation of what is being said. When we need to bring froth He will bring all things to our remembrance. There are some things that only Holy Spirit can teach us. We do learn from men and woman because we need information in order to exist here on earth. We spend many years in school from elementary through high school, for some of us through graduate school and for others it seems like school never ends because of the nature of our occupation or vocation. But John is letting us know that some things are taught by Holy Spirit and the anointing that He has given us is truth and it will also teach us all things:

1Jo 2:27 But the anointing which ye have received of him abideth in you, and ye need not that any man teach you: but as the same anointing teacheth you of all things, and is truth, and is no lie, and even as it hath taught you, ye shall abide in him. KJV

Chapter 5 – Birthing Spiritual Things with God

We have to create things in the spirit before they are manifested in the natural. We must realize that God wants us to birth spiritual things and that requires a more intimate relationship with Him. God sees us as producers. He created us from the dust of the ground (earth) which is capable of bringing forth. We are able to grow things in the spirit. God gives us ideas to birth, He gives us ministries to birth, He gives us visions to birth, missions to birth, businesses to birth because He has sent us all to earth on assignment. We all have a purpose for being here and our destiny is attached to our purpose.

We are to use the word of God (Jesus Christ is the word) as seed to produce anything that we need. Remember our physical body does physical birthing and we know that only females can do that physically, however as the bride of Christ all of us can birth spiritual things because there is no gender in Christ. There is only one bride of Christ and we can all do what the other can do we see that in *Gal 3:28 There is neither Jew nor Greek, there is neither bond nor free, there is neither male nor female: for ye are all one in Christ Jesus. KJV*

Things are produced in the spirit before they manifest in the natural. We have to speak words in order to come into what we desire. God will give us the desires of our hearts, because we are His children and He loves us. If we want to produce anything in the natural we must conceive it in the spirit first. God allows us to use our words and actions as seed, therefore we must be good stewards over our words even the words we speak over ourselves. God's plan for us to produce is perfect and we cannot change it for our convenience. If we want God's best we must recognize how we function and agree to grow spiritually so that we can grow spiritual things efficiently and effectively until they are birthed in the natural.

Now let us go to Mark chapter 4 and get an understanding of the mystery of the parable of the sower and the seed. We need to do this so that we can get an understanding of the function of the earth (ground). It says in:

Mark 4:3 Hearken; Behold, there went out a sower to sow: *The sower is sowing seed and the seed is the Word.*

The word is (in the person of Jesus Christ), we are the sowers and the ground (soil). This is our part we are positioned to bring forth the Word of God, which is the seed. Farmers know not to plant seed in bad soil, they know that they will not get an adequate harvest and sometimes no harvest at all in bad soil. They can almost look at the soil and know when it is good or bad.

That is how it should be with us. We should know when we have not cultivated our ground and cause it to become good ground. Every farmer knows that you have to prepare the ground so that it can bring forth the seed. Cultivation is the preparation process, you have to till or plow, if you do not have equipment to till or plow, then you get tools that will allow you to dig or hoe. That is breaking up the soil causing the soil to be soft and in addition you get rid of the residue still in the ground from last season's crops. Once you do that it makes it easy to plant a seed, after that you have to fertilize the soil to make sure that it has sufficient nutrients, because it may be weak from the last growing season. If necessary, use mulch with shrubs or trees and finally get rid of the weeds that take the opportunity to grow that you did not plant, because they choke the plants growing from the seeds you planted.

For us as ground that means that we have to study the word of God and be steadfast in what we have already learned. That helps us to get rid of things that are already there like bad habits, sin or anything that would make our ground hard. These things do not want to give up territory, but they have to because they cannot cohabitate with the word of God. As we begin to get rid of these things and begin to understand any particular principle in the word of God then we have to make that word a lifestyle and that keeps us strong and when we are strong in the word of God we welcome the tilling of our ground. We see that in:

Hsa 10:12 Sow to yourselves in righteousness, reap in mercy; break up your fallow ground: for it is time to seek the LORD, till he come and rain righteousness upon you.

The fallow ground is hard and you cannot plant in it unless it is plowed. If you drop the seed on the top of the ground it is not planted. The wind can come and blow it away, a bird or some other small animal will come by and eat it, and the rain may come and carry it to a creek or some other body of water. That is what happens to the Word of God when we plant it in untilled ground.

Let us take a look at one instance where the seed was planted in unplowed ground in:

Mark 4:4 And it came to pass, as he sowed, some fell by the way side, and the fowls of the air came and devoured it up.

You see what happened here the seed was not planted in the earth it was planted on top of the soil and there was no opportunity for growth. This is what we do when we have no depth of the Word of God in us. We try to continue to plant on untilled ground not understanding that it is not going to grow. Jesus explained this part of the parable in verse:

[15] And these are they by the way side, where the word is sown; but when they have heard, Satan cometh immediately, and taketh away the word that was sown in their hearts.

Satan was the fowl of the air that came and took away the word that was sown in their hearts.

Jesus goes on to explain what happens when you try to plant where there are stones in:

Mark 4:5 And some fell on stony ground, where it had not much earth; and immediately it sprang up, because it had no depth of earth.

This seed was planted in the earth but it was too shallow. It was not deep enough in the earth to be able to start a root system. If we do not avail ourselves and allow the word of God to be rooted and grounded in us then when a storm comes we cannot hold onto that tender plant that has no root system. All you need is a little heat to pressure us and we will give up and quit. We will give up that word and let it go especially when we do not like heat or pressure.

Jesus explains what happens in this:

Mark 4:6 But when the sun was up, it was scorched; and because it had no root, it withered away. 16 And these are they likewise which are sown on stony ground; who, when they have heard the word, immediately receive it with gladness; 17 And have no root in themselves, and so endure but for a time: afterward, when affliction or persecution ariseth for the word's sake, immediately they are offended.

Mark 4:7 And some fell among thorns, and the thorns grew up, and choked it, and it yielded no fruit.

Thorns choke the life out of plants by robbing them of the opportunity to coexist with them.

Jer 4:3 For thus saith the LORD to the men of Judah and Jerusalem, Break up your fallow ground, and sow not among thorns.

Any farmer or gardener knows to remove the thorns before planting seeds. If you live in the city you cannot imagine the thorns that are talked about in this passage. Thorns as mentioned here are not the thorns as we see them on a rose stem. These thorns are deadly and are not as we imagine them to be. I was speaking with one of my relatives who had firsthand experience with these types of thorns and she said that they are to be avoided at all costs. She said that she stepped on one and it completely pierced through her shoe, fortunately she felt it before it pieced her foot but she knows of someone who almost lost a body part because they were pierced by one of these thorns. They are difficult to remove and they cause infections quickly. You can see from the photo how long they are and they can completely pierce through some body parts. The thorns from this bush go in easy but they do not come out easy, when you pull them out they are very difficult to get out. Nothing can grow with them and they pierce very easily. Just like sin is easy to get in but hard to get out. They do not have to be pushed hard; any kind of pressure will cause them to pierce. This is the type that must have been placed on the head of Jesus. These thorns represent the cares of this world; the cares of this world will cause our seed to become unfruitful. They contaminate our ground. Notice what Jesus said in verses:

18 and 19 - And these are they which are sown among thorns; such as hear the word, ¹⁹ And the cares of this world, and the deceitfulness of riches, and the lusts of other things entering in, choke the word, and it becometh unfruitful

This is how you protect your ground by not letting the cares of this world stay in your ground, you have to plow them up and get them out. We cannot care about what the world cares about because all of these things are hidden in sin. We can overcome all of them because we are hidden in Christ.

Now that we understand how to properly prepare our ground, we can plant seed, because now we have good ground. Jesus mentions in:

Mark 4:8 And other fell on good ground, and did yield fruit that sprang up and increased; and brought forth, some thirty, and some sixty, and some an hundred. The seed was planted deep in the ground, received the light from Jesus Christ and water and wind from the ministry of the Holy Spirit.

Jesus had explained this process very well but it was not understood, therefore He explained it to those who wanted to be good earth (ground) and grow an abundance of spiritual things.

This is certainly a mystery. When Jesus explained this He was talking about the power of the earth and how much power God had put in His earthen vessels to grow, reproduce and give birth to spiritual things.

If you want to experience the fullness of the power of the earth then you have to pay attention to what Jesus said after he taught this parable to the multitudes.

After he taught the parable to the multitudes he said to them in:

Mark 4:9 And he said unto them, He that hath ears to hear, let him hear.

But some of them wanted to experience the power of the earth so they followed him and asked Him to explain what He had taught.

Mark 4:11-12 And he said unto them, Unto you it is given to know the <u>mystery of the kingdom of God: but unto them that are without, all these things are done in parables:</u> ¹² That seeing they may see, and not perceive; and hearing they may hear, and not understand; lest at any time they should be converted, and their sins should be forgiven them.

This is the KEY- the earth is already set up to produce and bring forth, therefore, anybody saved or unsaved can follow this process and be able to grow in the spiritual arena just as things are able to grow in the natural. So Jesus explained that knowing the answer to this mystery was not for every- one, but for those that are believers and followers of Jesus Christ. Jesus goes on to say in:

Mark 4:13 And he said unto them, Know ye not this parable? and how then will ye know all parables? Then He begin to expound on the mystery of the earth and the seed in verses 14-20.

This parable is based on the earth (ground) being good ground that is us and the seed which is the Word of God being sowed into our good ground. Jesus needs for us to understand about the earth and the power that is in the natural earth and that is in us that are formed from the earth. Once we understand how the earth works in the natural and how we work in the spiritual then we can understand all parables. With this understanding we can multiply the return on the word that the Lord has given us.

Chapter 6 – Growing Your Seed

The first thing that we have to do is to prepare our ground to be healthy. It is possible for us to allow our ground to be unhealthy to grow seed. Let us follow up with the 3 different unhealthy grounds for seed in the parable of the sower that we have to be aware of:

The way side – The Greek word for way side is **hodos** meaning a course of conduct or a way (i.e. manner) of thinking, feeling, deciding. If we let our mind wonder from the word of God in our thinking, actions or deeds we created an unhealthy environment for seed to grow in our ground. We cannot receive it if we do not understand it. How do we get to a position of not understanding? It is because our mind is a part of our soul and as we said earlier it does not know what to pray nor does it have the water and air that we need to grow that word. We need the ministry of Holy Spirit. We need to spend more time praying, asking for the involvement and help of Holy Spirit, more time fasting and more time studying the word of God so that we know what seeds to plant once we prepare our ground for the seed.

A stony place (ground) – The Greek word for Stony ground is **petrōdēs** meaning rocky, stony or a ground full of rocks. Seed cannot grow in rocks. We receive the word with joy but before it can develop a root system, the enemy sends persecution and tribulation after that word because he can't get the word out of you, because you have already received it so he sends persecution and tribulation hoping that you will get offended and prefer to deal with the offense and reject the word so you can get rid of the persecution and tribulation, rather than keeping the word and completing the process of dealing with persecution and tribulation as working in your favor for the benefit of the word received.

Many times we get offended because of our self-seeking fulfillment system. Many of us hate to be proven wrong and sometimes that is because we may have to admit it or quit it. In addition, we do not like being talked about negatively, we do not like being lied on, we do not like being dishonored, we do not like being left out and the list goes on and on. However, when we get offended by people we have made them our god. This was a very interesting lesson for me because I was seeking approval from people and none of them have a heaven or hell they can put me in yet I gave them the opportunity to rule over me by submitting to their attitudes, lifestyles and opinions of me. I know now that I have a choice and I no longer adhere to the systems that the enemy sends to me. Just in case you want to know how I did it, I am happy to report that it was Holy Spirit that did it, He helped me every step of the way. He helped me through many tears, hurts, heartaches and pain and I know that I could not have done it without Him.

Thorns – The Greek word for thorns is **akantha** meaning thorn, bramble bush, brier, or a thorny plant. This is an interesting one. I know you are asking just as I did "what are thorns in the spirit"? I did not understand and I wanted to know what the thorns in the spirit are. Well, they are the things we love more than God such as the care of this world, and the deceitfulness of riches. They choke the word that is already fruitful and causes it to become unfruitful. I remember when I accepted a big thorn. I had signed up for something that I saw in the word of God, but I had not come to the understanding that the earth is the Lord's, the fullness thereof and all of the inhabitants, therefore when the Devil came to me and said that I could not have what the word of God had promised me. I believed him and as a result I let that bad information choke the truth until it was no longer truth to me. It was still truth but not to me.

Again it was Holy Spirit that got me out of that jam. That was like a log jam on a river, you know the logs were put in the river to float down stream by the current to another destination, however when they jam they stop the transportation system of the river and create a dam. Now the river is not going to flow as before, its banks are going to overflow. Logs do not overflow; however, they are causing a problem for the river because they jammed together. Now, the river, nearby residents, animals and anything in close proximity to this accidental dam is in trouble. By that I mean much of the word of God that I tried to receive got choked behind the log jam. I was not sure if I was going to get anything from God, I knew people that were getting from God what I was asking for but somehow I thought God would not do it for me. How great was that log jam. All I can say now is thank you Holy Spirit for He is excellent in getting rid of log jams.

We can plant our seed by the way side, stony places or thorns. You say then how can I protect my ground from becoming unhealthy to grow seed? We do that by making sure that we hear and understand the word of God. Do not allow lack of understanding to be an option. Do not choose to love the cares of this world and riches more than God's word and by not being offended when persecution and tribulations come because of the word of God that you have received.

We are the sons of God, therefore, we start out with good ground (earth), the Greek word for ground in this passage is **gē** meaning arable land or the ground, the earth as a stand- ing place. The Greek word for good is **kalos** meaning beautiful, handsome, excellent, eminent, choice, surpassing, precious, useful, suitable, commendable, admirable, beautiful to look at, shapely, magnificent, good, excellent in its nature and characteristics, and therefore well adapted to its ends. If we receive seed in good ground, take a look at what God says we can have in:

Mat 13:23 But he that received seed into the good ground is he that heareth the word, and understandeth [it]; which also beareth fruit, and bringeth forth, some an hundred- fold, some sixty, some thirty.

This is a powerful principle; with good ground you can bring forth a multiplied harvest. Have you ever experience a multiplied harvest? If not prepare your ground and start receiving a multiplied harvest today.

Chapter 7 -
Rejoice and Be Glad

The great part about understanding what is going on with the seed is that nothing, no-thing, person, place, circumstance, situation, government or commercial entity can stop you as ground (earth) from growing your seed. We are encouraged to rejoice because The LORD reigns and HE is all powerful. He reigns and has rule over all that was, is, and ever shall be.

1 Ch 16:31 Let the heavens be glad, and let the earth rejoice: and let [men] say among the nations, The LORD reigneth.

We are not to have any concern that God's word will not prosper, because it will always work. Therefore, we should keep our confession and our physical and facial expressions in a place of expectancy and victory knowing that we can never lose when we plant the word of God in good ground.

If we follow the passages previously mentioned in Psalm 96 we see what is expected of everything that Jesus Christ reigns over. None of the gods that people worship in the earth can stop Jesus Christ because everything is subject to Him. Let us take a look at what is said to the people, heavens, the earth, the seas, the field and the trees of the earth rejoice and take note of the fact that the LORD requires that all worship Him in the beauty of His holiness. We are to sing His praises and give Him glory and strength. Because the LORD comes to judge the earth and He shall judge the world with righteousness and the people with truth, not facts because the word of God is the only truth there is or ever shall be.

We must worship God, rejoice and be glad and do not judge people even ourselves. God is not going to change His word because of our circumstances, situations, or conditions. Many times we are the victims of some sinful act that we had no control over and we feel that we have to take care of ourselves. However, God wants us to use His word to take care of everything thing that we have need of.

Many times when we see what other people have we want that. There is nothing wrong with that if it is aligned with the word of God, but many times it is not, because it is aligned with the world's system and the gods associated with that particular item or event. We want to have and do things that will cause us to line up with the gods of this world. I know that we want to justify things that do not celebrate God for various reasons but nothing is greater than God so we can be assured that when we plant the word of God (our seed) in our good ground that it is going to produce the harvest that we desire. To God be all of the honor and the glory, we do not give credit to our education, intellect, training, position, our clothes, or houses, cars or any other thing. Nor do we worship any of these things for the earth is the Lord's and we are also. We can see all of this in:

Psa 96:4-13 For great is the Lord and greatly to be praised; He is to be reverently feared and worshiped above all [so-called] gods. ⁵ For all the gods of the nations [are] idols: but the LORD made the heavens. ⁶ Honour and majesty [are] before him: strength and beauty [are] in his sanctuary. ⁷ Give unto the LORD, O ye kindreds of the people, give unto the LORD glory and strength. ⁸ Give unto the LORD the glory [due unto] his name: bring an offering, and come into his courts.⁹ O worship the LORD in the beauty of holiness: **fear before him, all the earth.** *¹⁰ Say among the heathen [that] the LORD reigneth: the world also shall be established that it shall not be moved: he shall judge the people righteously. 11 Let the heavens rejoice, and let the earth be glad; let the sea roar, and the fulness thereof. ¹² Let the field be joyful, and all that [is] therein: then shall all the trees of the wood rejoice ¹³ Before the LORD: for he cometh,* **for he cometh to judge the earth***: he shall judge the world with righteousness, and the people with his truth.*

Isaiah talks about another item that will help us with our ground growing process and that is to hear.

Isa 34:1 Come near, ye nations, to hear; and hearken, ye people: let the earth hear, and all that is therein; the world, and all things that come forth of it.

The phrase <u>to here</u> in the Hebrew is shama` and it means: to "hear, listen to, obey."

This is very important. We must purpose in our hearts to listen to the LORD and be obedient to His word because when He judges and proclaims the outcome nothing can escape. In this particular passage God is angry and He is talking about nothing shall escape the words He has spoken over that which He has judged. Remember what Jesus said to them after He explained the mystery of the sower and the seed. Mark 4:9 And he said unto them, He that hath ears to hear, let him hear.

What about the cares of this world? What are we to do with them because they can cause us not to have good ground? Nobody can take care of things like the LORD can. It is important that we understand that and allow God to be God and quit trying to take care of our cares. God wants to do that for us. He has admonished us to cast our cares on Him. If we do that we will not create unhealthy ground by giving attention to the cares of this world. We are not designed to carry the cares of this world and doing so would damage our ground and cause the word that was fruitful to be unfruitful. God said in His word cast your care on me and we can find that in:

1Pe 5:6-7 Humble yourselves therefore under the mighty hand of God, that he may exalt you in due time: ⁷ Casting all your care upon him; for he careth for you.

We must also be open to receive righteousness from the LORD, Isaiah talks about the earth being open and bringing forth salvation. Being open means to be free or to be loose, God has positioned us, the earth to bring forth as seen in Isa 45:8 Drop down, ye heavens, from above, and let the skies pour down righteousness: let the earth open, and let them bring forth (to bear fruit, be fruitful) salvation, and let righteousness spring up together (united together); I the LORD have created it.

We must understand the LORD has created everything. Nothing that was made was made without the word. Now if we think about that we can realize that we should not have an agenda of any kind. We should be free and open to receive the righteousness that the LORD is pouring into us to bear fruit and be fruitful and be saved from sin and everything that will ever confront us. This is what is said of Christ".

John 1:3 All things were made by him; and without him was not any thing made that was made.

God has given each one of us an assignment to complete in the earth. We did not send ourselves to the earth. Since we did not we cannot come up with an agenda of what we plan to do while we are here on earth. I always thought I knew exactly what I should or should not be doing. I had my own agenda, but I have realized that only what I do for God is what I should not neglect.

The reason that we were sent to the earth is called our vocation. We have a passion for doing that but most of us do not work in the area of our passion. What we do to make money to live is our occupation. God has given us a purpose for being here and we must embrace that first and not look at what we see and feel in the natural as a place of focus and not respond to our eternal purpose. Paul advises us in:

2Cr 4:18 While we look not at the things which are seen, but at the things which are not seen: for the things which are seen [are] temporal; but the things which are not seen [are] eternal.

It is easier for us to see ourselves as the world has taught us to see, but we must be an open vessel to receive the righteousness of God and be fruitful. We can do these things because the LORD reigns and He has created it all to work together. The fullness of the Godhead is in every believer and so is the power of the earth.

Chapter 8 – The Husbandman

What is a husbandman? Why do you and I (the earth) need a husbandman? We will talk about that later, but let us start at the beginning Jesus Christ did a wonderful thing for us, something that we take for granted. He became the spiritual ground (earth). He was man (the son of man) and God (the son of God) that we need to grow spiritual things. We cannot grow spiritual things without Him. We are hidden in Him and we also have received His blood and spiritual DNA.

Eph 3:9 KJV And to make all [men] see what [is] the fellowship of the mystery, which from the beginning of the world hath been hid in God, who created all things by Jesus Christ: AMP

Everything was created by and for Christ Jesus, since that is so, how powerful must the earth be that we are hidden in the one that created it. Therefore we have access to the power of the earth that we cannot even imagine.

We do not have to be concerned about what is in us to create and grow things but stay focused on what is in Him, as we know according to:

Jhn 1:3 KJV All things were made by him; and without him was not any thing made that was made.

When you look at soil (dirt, ground, earth) there is nothing attractive about it, but beautiful flowers grow up out of it. This is great to me because the ground that Jesus has given us is all powerful, it has all the ingredients in it that is needed to grow spiritual things, it has no sin in it, therefore we are free from sin busting plants, when any of that is found in our ground all we have to do is repent and it is gone forever. It is the best soil ever because the one who created it is the soil. Anything that we could have possibly brought to the table is covered by the blood of Jesus and we are dead to it. Our life is hidden in Him the best ground possible. There is no greater ground than that of Christ.

Col 3:3 For ye are dead, and your life is hid with Christ in God. KJV

If we know that Jesus Christ is the ground that we are hidden in then who is the husbandman? Jesus made that very clear in:

John 15:1 KJV I am the true vine, and my Father is the husbandman.

Jesus is our husband but the Father is the husbandman. According to Merriam-Webster Dictionary a husbandman is one that plows and cultivates land, a farmer. This is very interesting because we have already talked about plowing and cultivating the land and now we know that we cannot do it for ourselves, we need God the Father to do that. In order for us to continue to be good ground we must stay connected to the vine, the vine is Jesus Christ and He is good ground. All we have to do is be obedient to the word of God, we do not have to make sure that we start with good ground, God does that, nor do we have to farm the word of God (seed), God does that. Once again we see in John 15:1-16 I am the True Vine, and My Father is the Vinedresser. AMP the first step is connect to the vine and stay connected. The Greek word for Vinedresser is geōrgos and the meaning of the word is a husbandman, tiller of the soil, a vine dresser.

Jesus uses this chapter to explain how this entire process works. We are designed to bring forth and bear fruit. We see in verse 2 the work of the husbandman and we find out what happens to the ground under both circumstances of bringing forth fruit or not bringing forth fruit.

Verse 2 Any branch in Me that does not bear fruit [that stops bearing] He cuts away (trims off, takes away); and He cleanses and repeatedly prunes every branch that continues to bear fruit, to make it bear more and richer and more excellent fruit. AMP

Remember all of those things that we needed to get rid of in bad ground, unhealthy soil? The Father is taking care of that for us, if we are willing and obedient to the ministry of the Holy Spirit. There is always a new level of growth that we must aspire to, we must bring forth and produce more, if we decide not to do that we will be cut off from the good ground of the true vine.

Notice what Jesus said in verse 3-4:

You are cleansed and pruned already, because of the word which I have given you [the teachings I have discussed with you]. ⁴ Dwell in Me, and I will dwell in you. [Live in Me, and I will live in you.] Just as no branch can bear fruit of itself without abiding in (being vitally united to) the vine, neither can you bear fruit unless you abide in Me. AMP

Remember we talked about being united with the good ground and that we cannot bring forth without Jesus Christ, Holy Spirit and the Father. We need all three in order to experience the fullness of the power of the earth as our spiritual ground.

Many of us have been praying asking God for particular things, we are trying to bring forth certain things but we do not see the results manifested in the natural as we had expected. One of the reasons is because we have not embraced verse 5:

I am the Vine; you are the branches. Whoever lives in Me and I in him bears much (abundant) fruit. However, apart from Me [cut off from vital union with Me] you can do nothing. AMP

The KJV of this verse says bringeth forth much fruit: God wants us to bring forth, but we have to be positioned to do that. This kind of activity is reserved for those who are the sons of God and Jesus Christ is the only avenue for that to be possible: How does this happen?

This is the first criteria; we must be born again in Christ. This is a key factor for your earth to produce as it should, without being connected to Christ you can do nothing.

The second thing that you have to do is stay connected, dwell in Jesus, the vine. If we do not stay connected we will be thrown out of the system of God's good ground and now men can treat us like fire wood and burn us up. When I talk to some folks they constantly tell me how tired they are and it seems that they are always on the edge of burnout. Then I speak with others who have similar rigorous schedules and they seem to always have the energy that they need to keep going even further. I noticed that the ones who have the energy to keep going depend on God to keep going and the others depend on themselves to keep going. Notice in verse 6 that it is men that gather you and burn you up not God.

verse 6 If a person does not dwell in Me, he is thrown out like a [broken-off] branch, and withers; such branches are gathered up and thrown into the fire, and they are burned. AMP.

The third thing that you have to do is allow the word of God to remain in you and continue to live in your heart you can not only bring forth fruit but you can ask for what you want. All of this is mentioned in:

verse 7 If you live in Me [abide vitally united to Me] and My words remain in you and continue to live in your hearts, ask whatever you will, and it shall be done for you. AMP Remember when Jesus said in ***Mat 15:18 But those***

things which proceed out of the mouth come forth from the heart; and they defile the man. **KJV** this lets us know that the mouth will speak what is in the heart and when you allow the word to remain in you and continue in your heart that is what is going to come out of your mouth. Jesus said in the parable of the sower (Luke 8:11 Now the parable is this: The seed is the word of God.) that the seed was the word of God and it is the word of God that is remaining in your heart. Then the words that come out of your mouth are seed, the harvest of which you can bring forth.

In addition Jesus says doing this is how you prove yourself to be a true follower of His, also that the Father is honored and glorified when we produce much fruit. The fact that Jesus loves us goes without saying because He did for us just because He loved us, but He still took the opportunity to explain this in:

verse [8] *When you bear (produce) much fruit, My Father is honored and glorified, and you show and prove yourselves to be true followers of Mine.* AMP and verse [9] *I have loved you, [just] as the Father has loved Me; abide in My love [[a]continue in His love with Me].* AMP

Finally Jesus gives instructions on how to keep this flowing forever. He lets us know that we are His friends and that He has chosen us so there was nothing that we should or could do to get Him to do this for us. Not only does God want us to bring forth fruit He wants it to remain. Jesus lets us know that He has kept nothing from us, that

He has said everything that the Father said to Him. Jesus wants us to understand that we are the sons of God and joint heirs with Him. He goes on to explain all of this in:

verses 10-16 If you keep My commandments [if you continue to obey My instructions], you will abide in My love and live on in it, just as I have obeyed My Father's commandments and live on in His love. [11] I have told you these things, that My joy and delight may be in you, and that your joy and gladness may be of full measure and complete and overflowing. [12] This is My commandment: that you love one another [just] as I have loved you. [13] No one has greater love [no one has shown stronger affection] than to lay down (give up) his own life for his friends. [14] You are My friends if you keep on doing the things which I command you to do. [15] I do not call you servants (slaves) any longer, for the servant does not know what his master is doing (working out). But I have called you My friends, because I have made known to you every- thing that I have heard from My Father. [I have revealed to you everything that I have learned from Him.] [16] You have not chosen Me, but I have chosen you and I have appointed you [I have planted you], that you might go and bear fruit and keep on bearing, and that your fruit may be lasting [that it may remain, abide], so that whatever you ask the Father in My Name [as [b]presenting all that I Am], He may give it to you. AMP

Chapter 9 – Holy Spirit Our Enabler and Our Helper

If you have ever done something really large by yourself then you know how important it is to have help. Jesus understood that His followers were going to need help after He left. Jesus understood that He was their Savior, Lord, King and help. He knew that He was God with us but to sustain and maintain they would need God in us. He knew that they would need the ministry of Holy Spirit and He knew that His disciples did not understand why at that time, so He began to tell them what was going to happen in:

John 14:16 And I will ask the Father, and He will give you another Comforter (Counselor, Helper, Intercessor, Advocate, Strengthener, and Standby), that He may remain with you forever—AMP

Have you ever felt like God was no longer with you or that He would not help you because of something you did, did not do or for whatever reason? This verse should free you from that feeling forever because for believers there are no conditions attached to receiving our Comforter, Counselor, Helper, Intercessor, Advocate, Strengthener and Standby who is in the person of Holy Spirit and He will be with us forever.

I wonder how many of us really understand the tenderness or the strength of Holy Spirit. I can remember not obeying when He told me to do something (my parents would not have tolerated that), yet He did and He kept teaching me. I can remember quenching His urging and doing just the opposite but He still kept me through it all. I remember being sad about some things and all of a sudden He would start laughter and that laughter would bubble up and out of me and I would find myself laughing also. The first time that this happened I did not know if He was laughing at me or with me but now I know He was laughing so that I would know that He knew best what season or what moment we were in. Soon I began to realize that He wanted me to change my countenance, because it was a time of rejoicing not a time of sorrow. We have a more intimate relationship now and He can just tell me "this is not a worse case situation" and I know to change my countenance.

I love to talk about Holy Spirit, He is my best friend and I talk to Him all the time. I said that to say that I was doing more talking than listening at first but He still listened. I did not get the answers that I would have gotten if I had listened more but He met me where I was at that time. I am still working on listening but I listen much more now than I use to.

When I think of Him as being my Comforter I cannot count the times when I was certain that everybody hated me, that was not true but I thought it was at the time, even in this time of very bad thinking Holy Spirit would always send one person in the midst of what seemed like an unbearable storm to comfort me. He helped me out of so many situations even when I was the reason that I was having the problem. He did that not to agree with my wrong doing but because I asked Him to help me not do any more wrong trying to fix that wrong.

Some of us my still think that we can make it through life on our own but I know that I cannot, I need Holy Spirit in every area of my life. Jesus knew that too, therefore He pre- pared them to receive Emmanuel God in them.

Jesus continued to talk to them about Holy Spirit as being the Spirit of Truth in:

John 14:17 The Spirit of Truth, Whom the world cannot receive (welcome, take to its heart), because it does not see Him or know and recognize Him. But you know and recognize Him, for He lives with you [constantly] and will be in you.

This is so important because when we examine what this means we can have complete confidence that no matter what the situation or circumstance He knows the correct answer and we cannot be fooled. The word truth in this verse is the Greek word **alētheia** which means what is true in any matter under consideration.

We know that Satan is the author of lies, therefore we can expect to be lied on or to at some point in time. But with the Spirit of Truth we will always know what is going on that it is true no matter what we think about it. Now if you ever have to wonder if God, Holy Spirit is helping you if you are trying to take care of a situation by not telling the truth, I can help you, He is not because He is the Spirit of Truth. To understand this better we have to go back to:

John 14:6 Jesus saith unto him, I am the way, the truth, and the life: no man cometh unto the Father, but by me. KJV

Where Jesus explained that He is the way, the truth and the life, when we focus on truth we know that Jesus Christ is also the word of God and therefore He is the only truth there is and He is the only way there is to get to God the Father. Now we can understand how the Godhead, Father, Son (Christ) and Holy Spirit work together. Holy Spirit is not going to lead us, guide us, help us, comfort us, keep us or do anything for us that does not line up with the word of God.

In addition, to having Him, Holy Spirit Jesus explains in this same verse that the world cannot receive Holy Spirit. They do not see Him nor do they know Him and the reason for that is what we have just explained in verse 6, you must be a born again believer, you must come through Jesus Christ, then and only then do you get Holy Spirit as Jesus has promised.

We don't even have to be concerned about the world knowing what we know because they cannot receive, see or know Holy Spirit. All we have to do is yield to the ministry of Holy Spirit and He will guide us into all truth. You will never be surprised. Let me say also, that you must be able to handle the truth. If you are able to handle what Holy Spirit has to say, He will only say what you can handle.

However, He will keep teaching and training until you mature more in Christ, then He can say what He could not say before. This is a continuous process. Some of us cannot handle information that is the truth about ourselves, we are in denial. People know some things that we cannot see, they can tell what's going on with us by what we say or do, but if we are in denial we don't know that they know, but when we make it a practice to yield to Holy Spirit's ministry on a continuous basis He will lead us into that truth about ourselves also.

Then Jesus closes verse 17 by saying He will be in you. Now we don't have to wonder if He is with us nor do we have to ponder about where He is because He is in us.

The next thing that Jesus said to them is even more exciting, He said in verses 18-20 "I will not leave you comfortless, I will come to you" now he comforts them by letting them know that He is not going to leave them alone to work things out for themselves. He has already told them that they can do nothing without Him and now is talking about leaving and sending another comforter and letting them know that there is going to come a time when they will know that He is in his Father, they are in Him and He in them. The Amplified version of those verses is:

¹⁸ I will not leave you as orphans [comfortless, desolate, bereaved, forlorn, helpless]; I will come [back] to you. ¹⁹ Just a little while now, and the world will not see Me any more, but you will see Me; because I live, you will live also. ²⁰ At that time [when that day comes] you will know [for yourselves] that I am in My Father, and you [are] in Me, and I [am] in you. AMP

This is the exciting part, God the Father, Son and Holy Spirit are one. They coexist together, therefore when Holy Spirit comforter comes He has access to the Son and the Father. Remember Jesus said earlier that when the comforter comes He will never leave us. That means that the Father nor the Son will ever leave us. We know now that we have access to all three via the Holy Spirit.

One part that has been difficult for some of us is the understanding that we can do nothing without Jesus Christ. He made it possible for us to have good ground, because we are using His good ground. He made it possible for us to be free of the penalty of sin and now we can grow spiritual things without hindrance, He made it possible for us to be free of the power of sin and now we can plant the word of God which is the seed that Jesus was talking about in the parable and we will always get a good crop free of death. He made it possible for us to come into the presence of God and since He is God we can become members of the family of God if we come through Him.

If we were to admit that without Him we could do nothing it would cause us not to think too highly of ourselves. God has positioned us in His family and he allows us to use His

Name, His Power, His Word and He makes available to us all that we need to accomplish our assignment in the earth.

The other part that has been a problem for some is that we can only think of ourselves as human. Yes we are humans but not just human. God created us in His image and as His likeness and gave us the assignment of managing the earth, but in our minds we do not see ourselves as overcomers, victorious, a chosen nation or royal priesthood. All we know is that we can't do this or we can't do that, therefore doing things like healing the sick is outside of our thought process.

As Jesus continues to tell them what must be done in order to keep their part of the covenant it seems too simple. All He asked for them to do is obey His words, and love Him. Of course obedience to Him is proof of our love for Him.

Remember what Jesus said in verses 25-26:

I have told you these things while I am still with you. 26 But the Comforter (Counselor, Helper, Intercessor, Advocate, Strengthener, Standby), the Holy Spirit, Whom the Father will send in My name [in My place, to represent Me and act on My behalf], He will teach you all things. And He will cause you to recall (will remind you of, bring to your remembrance) everything I have told you. AMP

Jesus knew that they would be troubled without Him and He prepared them to receive what was available to them. Imagine not even having to remember everything, the

Holy Spirit will bring back to their memory all that Jesus has taught them. Jesus not only reminded them of the help that He was sending but also the kind of help that they would be getting from the ministry of Holy Spirit.

Jesus is now ready for them to settle whatever they need to settle concerning what is about to happen. He wanted them to receive His peace and He gave them an explanation of what the peace that He has given them was all about in verses 27-31:

Peace I leave with you; My [own] peace I now give and bequeath to you. Not as the world gives do I give to you. Do not let your hearts be troubled, neither let them be afraid. [Stop allowing yourselves to be agitated and disturbed; and do not permit yourselves to be fearful and intimidated and cowardly and unsettled.] [28] You heard Me tell you, I am going away and I am coming [back] to you. If you [really] loved Me, you would have been glad, because I am going to the Father; for the Father is greater and mightier than I am. [29] And now I have told you [this] before it occurs, so that when it does take place you may believe and have faith in and rely on Me. [30] I will not talk with you much more, for the prince (evil genius, ruler) of the world is coming. And he has no claim on Me. [He has nothing in common with Me; there is nothing in Me that belongs to him, and he has no power over Me.] [31] But [[d]Satan is coming and] I do as the Father has commanded Me, so that the world may know (be convinced) that I love the Father and that

I do only what the Father has instructed Me to do. [I act in full agreement with His orders.] Rise, let us go away from here.

This passage is very interesting to me, because most of the people do not pay attention to Jesus' command to them which is appropriate for us today. He said stop allowing yourselves to be agitated and disturbed; and do not permit yourselves to be fearful, intimidated, cowardly and unsettled and in this same passage He tells them I need you to obey me in this because this is what will keep you safe. I am telling you in advance so that you will know what to expect and recognize it and when it comes you will believe, have faith and know that you can rely on Me.

Now this is a key to remember, Jesus says that I will not be talking much more therefore you have to remember what I have told you because Satan is coming and even though, he is an evil genius he has no claim on Me. He has nothing in common with Me; there is nothing in Me that belongs to him, and he has no power over Me. Then He told them I do as the Father has commanded Me, so that the world may know (be convinced) that I love the Father and that I do only what the Father has instructed Me to do. I act in full agreement with His orders. Now they know that He is not asking them to do something that He is not doing. It is important that we understand what it means for us not to have anything on us that Satan can claim, that we have nothing in common with him and that we have nothing in us that belongs to him and finally that he has no power over us.

We know that Jesus has freed us from the penalty and the power of sin, but we have to be willing to let Holy Spirit our Comforter help us get rid of the things that we may have in common with Satan, things like unforgiveness, strife, and envy, we must also have nothing in us that Satan can touch, because those are the things that he can use for his benefit. Many times those things are in us but we had nothing to do with what happened to cause the problem, it may have happened when we were a child it may be a generational curse but we have Holy Spirit and He will help us with all things.

We all have things that are not in agreement with the word of God that we need to get rid of and sometimes they may seem insignificant but God sees it all, for instance, worry, fear, doubt and unbelief, low self-worth etc. I don't know about you but I have heard some Christians explain things that are big sins are different from things that are small sins, well there are no big or small sins they are all sin. There are no little white lies, they are all lies and even though we would like to think that people who have visible sins like adultery are different from those that are sins done in secret like pornography. Even if we do not know what to pray for or what to ask for help with we can be comforted because Jesus sent us help in that area also, Paul mentioned that in:

Rom 8:26 Likewise the Spirit also helpeth our infirmities: for we know not what we should pray for as we ought: but the Spirit itself maketh intercession for us with groanings which cannot be uttered KJV.

We have a WIN-WIN situation here on earth; God has covered everything that we could possibly encounter. Satan is defeated and we are free from the power of sin and the penalty of sin all we need to do is seek the Lord's help and to make sure that we have all the help we needed He sent us Holy Spirit when he left. We do not have to fear anybody or anything else because God did not give us fear, He gave us a helper that cannot be defeated we see that in:

Heb 13:6 So that we may boldly say, The Lord [is] my helper, and I will not fear what man shall do unto me.

Now you may be wondering why we have to deal with sin at all if we are so free, it is because we are not yet free from the presence of sin, and because of that God has given us everything that we need in order to win every time.

Jesus said that He was in full agreement with what the Father has commanded Him to do and He does what the Father tells Him to do so that the world may know that He loves the Father. That lets us know that if we do what Jesus Christ who is the word of God told us to do that would indicate that we love Him and because we love He we also love the Father and Holy Spirit Remember that we said earlier that Holy Spirit lives in us as Paul mentions in:

1Co 6:19 What? know ye not that your body is the temple of the Holy Ghost [which is] in you, which ye have of God, and ye are not your own? KJV

And since He is in us we take Him everywhere we go, He is always present to help us if we would yield to His ministry. He is truly our enabler because He is the one doing the work. He is the one with the power and all He wants us to do is ask for His help.

Chapter 10 – The Mystery of the Earthen Vessel

(2 Co 4:7 KJV) But we have this treasure in earthen vessels, that the excellency of the power may be of God, and not of us.

An earthen vessel is a plain ordinary clay vessel. We of course were made from the dust of the earth and continue to be shaped be the potters (God's) hand. What makes the earth vessel that we live in so powerful? It is the power of God, we like to give too much credit to ourselves for this or for that but in fact none of the credit belongs to us. In fact we must also remember that we did not create ourselves so we can take no responsibility for that either.

Many times we get challenged by people that want to determine how good or bad we are, but they did not create any of us either, God is our only creator, He said that what he created was not only good but very good.

Gen 1:31 And God saw every thing that he had made, and, behold, [it was] very good. And the evening and the morning were the sixth day. KJV

One thing that I am convinced of is that we use the word good too loosely. We must understand what good is and the nature of it before we can release all the things that would prevent us from growing things in the spirit. Jesus said what good was but I don't think many of us paid attention. He said to a person that was addressing Him as good master that no one is good but God.

Mar 10:18 And Jesus said unto him, Why callest thou me good? [there is] none good but one, [that is], God. KJV

The word good in the Hebrew is towb meaning:

(good, pleasant, agreeable, ethical, a good thing, benefit, welfare, benefit, good things, prosperity, happiness).

The Greek the word for good is **agathos** meaning:

(of good constitution or nature, useful, salutary, good, pleasant, agreeable, joyful, happy, excellent, distinguished, upright, honorable), therefore from this we know that one of the characteristics of God is Good. None of us can qualify by nature as good. However, we can qualify through Jesus Christ.

Remember, what Paul said to the Romans, we are hidden in Christ:

Rom 12:5 So we, [being] many, are one body in Christ, and every one members one of another. KJV

and we know that Christ the Son, is God, He is the word of God and was with God in the beginning. Now we understand that Good can only be defined as who God is, God is not good just because something good has happened to us, as many of us say "God is Good", He is good because we cannot define good without looking at who God is and He is good.

Since we are hidden in Christ then it is His ground that we use to grow things, He has all of the ingredients that we need. We cannot qualify to grow good things without Him. We have no control over the ability of our ground to grow things, God took care of that, but we do have a will that can choose to plant good seed, the word of God.

You cannot grow good things if you are not saved; I have had a few people tell me that they were good people when I asked them about being saved. They did not understand that good is not possible for us without God, because God is the definition of good, since God is the definition of good you can literally say have a good day and not understand that you really mean have a God day.

People think that they are good because of their ability to discipline themselves. They can learn how to act in public, they can learn civil laws and obey them, they can learn how to control their emotions, and they can learn how not to be rude in the long grocery store lines etc., that is not the nature of being good. Good is defined by the righteousness of God, good is God. Isaiah explains it this way:

Isa 64:6 But we are all as an unclean [thing], and all our righteousnesses [are] as filthy rags; and we all do fade as a leaf; and our iniquities, like the wind, have taken us away. KJV.

People who think that they are good without God do not realize that they would have to not commit any sin in thought, word or deed from their conception in the womb until we leave the planet earth. We know that is not possible, therefore we know that our nature is not naturally good and we need the salvation that Jesus Christ has provided for us. With that salvation, all things are possible because nothing is greater than God who provides our salvation.

Our earthen vessel is a great mystery, how can we be born in this natural vessel with no power and then be born again unto God and have all of His power? This is certainly a mystery if we do not understand what God did in His creation of man and His salvation of man. As we mentioned earlier, the first Adam (man) was created from a natural source, the dirt of the earth, which was his earth suit (shell) that connected him with natural earth, but when God blew the breath of life into him, he became a living soul.

Gen 2:7 And the LORD God formed man [of] the dust of the ground, and breathed into his nostrils the breath of life; and man became a living soul. KJV

Now he has his spirit living in the shell with the image and likeness of God being a part of that spirit. Remember, the shell had no life when it was created it was formed from the same substance that was called earth but now that it has life in it that part is called his spirit man. The original intent of God and still is that the shell be controlled by the spirit man.

Remember that the shell had no life in the beginning and is dependent on what control system will give it direction. Our physical body is given direction by our soul which is in touch with our flesh or our spirit man which is in touch with God. When we are born in the natural we are born after the likeness of the first Adam, the natural man, of which we have no choice in the matter.

We cannot choose our parents, our sex or the time that we are born, but the second birth into the family of God we get to choose. When we make that choice we are born after the likeness of the second Adam Jesus Christ which is a spiritual birth not a natural one. It is this birth that we do not get the magnitude of what has happened to us as believers in Christ. It may seem like things would be easy once we come into the family of God and they are if we obey God, however, the closer you get to God the more you have to keep the enemy in his place. The fight is on because the enemy does not like to lose, therefore you have to know who you are in God.

If you are a believer in Jesus Christ then you know that we have an enemy Satan, who is a defeated foe. We also know that we are free from the penalty of sin, free from the power of sin but not free from the presence of sin, therefore we are going to have to fight from time to time for ourselves and for others. You may be asking "if he is defeated, why do we have to fight?" It is because many of us lack the knowledge or the spiritual maturity of his defeated position. We know also that the people of God are destroyed for the lack of knowledge and rejection of knowledge.

Hos 4:6 My people are destroyed for lack of knowledge: because thou hast rejected knowledge, I will also reject thee, that thou shalt be no priest to me: seeing thou hast forgotten the law of thy God, I will also forget thy children. KJV

God gives us instructions in Ephesians 6 about how to prepare for the attack of the enemy and He gives us amour to fight with. The interesting thing is that the only offense we have is the word of God all of the rest of the amour is used for defense. Since the word of God is our only offense we must be able to plant it in good ground in order to get the harvest promised of thirty, sixty or a hundred fold. However, there are some things that we have to consider and get rid of and to do that we need the help and power of Holy Spirit to help to deal with those things.

Now that we understand that the earth suit, the shell that our spirit man lives in we should also remember that our body is the temple of God and we are a vessel in a great house and we have to make sure that we are a vessel of honor. Paul explained this to Timothy in:

2 Ti 2:20 But in a great house there are not only vessels of gold and of silver, but also of wood and of earth; and some to honour, and some to dishonour. KJV

Being a vessel of honor prepares you to be used by Holy Spirit.

God gave us a great example of this in the Old Testament with the symbolism of the tabernacle and the temple of God. We needed to be completely holy in order to be the temple of God. Jesus Christ made that possible. It is also important that we understand what God is requiring of us as believers, and one of those requirements is to be holy as He is holy. We could never do that on our own, but in Christ we can. It was Jesus that made it possible for us to live eternally with God and also for God to be able to live in us.

All of this is necessary, because of the appointed destiny of every believer, that being each person in the body of Christ. On the way to our destination we sometimes get weary of the journey because of the stringent process and the Holy requirement.

Our journey begins with God; therefore, living in His presence is where we all want to be. God is not waiting for us to do anything to qualify to become a member of the family of God, all we have to do is believe that Jesus Christ is God and has been raised from the dead and is the first among the living. God planned for us to be the temple of God from the beginning.

Let us follow the symbolism of the tabernacle and the temple just to get a glimpse of what God shared with the Old Testament saints that we now enjoy as New Testaments saints.

God showed us the end at the beginning and He used the tabernacle and the temple as types and symbols to help us understand what Jesus did for us in this regard, His sacrifice made it possible for us to qualify to become the sanctuary of God.

Going from the Outer Court to the Holy of Holies is very important for Christians today because some of us will not be able to do what is expected of us today if we do not go into the Holy of Holies and stay there. The purpose of the tabernacle and the temple in the Old Testament was to have a place for God to dwell among us.

God wanted a place to dwell among His people and He shared this with Moses in Exodus 28:8. God gave Moses the instructions for the tabernacle, which at that time had to be a moveable sanctuary, but later Solomon built the temple using the same blueprint that God had given to Moses for the tabernacle. Each contained an outer court, a holy place and the holy of holies. Each of these had a door that led to the next and each was symbolic of what God had in for us today as the temple or sanctuary of God. Note the following symbolism of each:

The Outer Court was the first door, it was the place where God and man worked together with man cooperating with God. In this section there was a Brazen altar lifted up higher than the others and was used to burn and sacrifice the animals, in particular the blood of the sin offering was used to cover the sin of the owner, the owner was to lay his hand on the head of his offering and transfer his sin to the lamb and the lamb became his sin offering, thus it died for the owner and it's blood covered the sin, this was symbolic of what Jesus Christ did for us. We see that in:

Lev 17:11 For the life of the flesh [is] in the blood: and I have given it to you upon the altar to make an atonement for your souls: for it [is] the blood [that] maketh an atonement for the soul. KJV.

The other item that we want to mention was the Brazen Laver where the priest has to wash their hands and feet before service and it was located before the entrance of the next door. The Outer Court is a place of God's visitation.

The Holy Place was the second door; this was the place where God was working through man, in other words man and God working together as we do now in the church. This section has three pieces of furniture in it:

The Golden altar of Incense positioned just before the Veil (the next door) and was used to burn incense unto the Lord, this was a sweet savor to the Lord, and the incense speaks of prayer, praise and intercession.

The Table of Shewbread which is significant of the Lord Jesus Christ Himself as the Bread of Life to the people.

The Golden Candlestick, the purpose of the candlestick was to give light to illumine all that was in the sanctuary and symbolizes the light of the church, remember we are now the sanctuary where Holy Spirit resides, remember that Jesus is the light of the world and He has given that to us ***John 8:12 Then spake Jesus again unto them, saying, I am the light of the world: he that followeth me shall not walk in darkness, but shall have the light of life*** and in ***Mat 5:14 Ye are the light of the world. A city that is set on an hill cannot be hid.***

The Holy of Holies, in the Holy of Holies it is all God. This is the place of God's presence. God's Shekinah Glory is found in the Holy of Holies. It is God's place of habitation on earth. It contains the Ark of the Covenant and it contained:

The tablets of the law, this is a type of the Father, the lawgiver and is symbolic of supreme authority of moral law, civil law, and ceremonial law.

The golden pot of manna which represents a type of Jesus Christ as the Bread of Life, the bread from heaven upon which the children of Israel fed for forty years in the wilderness, it is also symbolic of the word of God of which we feed on today.

Aaron's rod that budded represents one rod, one God, the bud being the Father as the source and the beginning, the flower as the Son fragrant and crushed and the fruit as the Holy Spirit fruitfulness. Also, the fullness of Jesus Christ as described in ***John 14:6 Jesus saith unto him, I am the way, the truth, and the life: no man cometh unto the Father, but by me. KJV.*** He is The Bud representing the way, He is Manna representing the truth and He is the rod representing life.

With all of this in mind we can imagine the greatness that God had in mind concerning the temple (sanctuary) where He would dwell, the fullness of the Godhead is in Jesus Christ and it is also in us. Paul explained this in:

Col 2:8-9 Beware lest any man spoil you through philosophy and vain deceit, after the tradition of men, after the rudiments of the world, and not after Christ. 9 For in him dwelleth all the fulness of the Godhead bodily. KJV

The Greek word for bodily is ***sōmatikōs*** which means:

Bodily, corporally of the exalted spiritual body, visible only to the inhabitants of heaven.

This word is used only once but this is a powerful message to the body of Christ. How many of us can say that we understand that the fullness of the Godhead is in us.

The Greek word for fullness in this verse is ***plērōma*** meaning:

That which is (has been) filled, a ship inasmuch as it is filled (i.e. manned) with sailors, rowers, and soldiers in the NT, the body of believers, as that which is filled with the presence, power, agency, riches of God and of Christ that which fills or with which a thing is filled of those things which a ship is filled, freight and merchandise, sailors, oarsmen, soldiers completeness or fullness of time fullness, abundance a fulfilling, keeping.

The mystery of the earth vessel that we live in is amazing not only can we grow things in the spirit but we have the Godhead helping us do it. If we only understood that God is doing all the work it would be much easier for us to let things go and let God do it. Remember the word "let" is giving someone permission to do something, we have to give God permission we cannot do what needs to be done on our own anyway, why not let God do what He does best and that is to be God.

It is very important that we understand what kind of vessel we are because often times we think that we are one kind of vessel and in reality we are another. We mentioned earlier that being a vessel of honor positions us to be used by the Holy Spirit, but are we vessels of horror or vessels of dishonor.

Paul talks to Timothy about the different kinds of vessels that exist in a great house so that we can determine what kind we are and we can also know the benefits of each positive and negative. In order to be fit and ready for any good work growing and bringing forth spiritual things we must be vessels of honor. How to become a vessel of honor or dishonor, not fit for any good work is found in:

> *2 Ti 2:20-21 But in a great house there are not only vessels of gold and silver, but also [utensils] of wood and earthenware, and some for honorable and noble [use] and some for menial and ignoble [use]. [21] So whoever cleanses himself [from what is ignoble and unclean, who separates himself from contact with contaminating and corrupting influences] will [then himself] be a vessel set apart and useful for honorable and noble purposes, consecrated and profitable to the Master, fit and ready for any good work AMP.*

Many of us know that we were not vessels of honor before we were saved. We know what we did and some of us are still working through some of those things with the help of God. However, there are some that believe that they are good people. Remember we mentioned what Jesus said in that regard no one is good except God. My daughter helped me with this some time ago. We were talking about how good God is and how often Christians say that when some- thing good happens to them. Especially when they have a praise report about something good that happened that they had been praying for, or they would get free of some troubling situations or people. The first thing they say is "God is good" because of the good thing that happened to them.

She said that she put a question before God about that and He gave her the understanding that she needed. God let her know that He is not good because something good happens to His people or anyone. He is good because good who He is. You cannot define "good" without God because good is only found in Him and it comes from Him, He is the definition of good. He is literally good. Good is who He is, therefore it is not possible for anyone else to be good. The next time you hear someone say "God is good" remember "Good is God" that is one of His names, He is Jehovah Good.

The Devil is also putting out snares to keep people from becoming vessels of honor, therefore Paul gives Timothy the information that he needs to give the people so that they will not be caught in the snare.

If we do not follow these instructions we may be caught in the Devil's snares also. Instructions are found in:

2 Ti 2:22-26 *__Shun youthful lusts__ and flee from them, and __aim at and pursue righteousness__ (all that is virtuous and good, right living, conformity to the will of God in thought, word, and deed); [and aim at and pursue] __faith, love__, [and] __peace__ (harmony and concord with others) __in fellowship with all [Christians], who call upon the Lord out of a pure heart.__ ²³ But __refuse__ (shut your mind against, have nothing to do with) __trifling__ (ill-informed, unedifying, stupid) __controversies over ignorant questionings__, for you know that they foster strife and breed quarrels. 24 And __the servant of the Lord must not be quarrelsome__ (fighting and contending). Instead, he __must be kindly to everyone__ and __mild-tempered__*

[preserving the bond of peace]; he <u>must be</u> <u>a skilled and suitable teacher</u>, <u>patient</u> and forbearing and <u>willing to suffer wrong</u>. 25 He must <u>correct his opponents</u> <u>with courtesy and gentleness</u>, in the hope that God may grant that they will repent and come to know the Truth [that they will perceive and recognize and become accurately acquainted with and acknowledge it], 26 And that they may come to their senses [and] escape out of the snare of the devil, having been held captive by him, [henceforth] to do His [God's] will. AMP

This is exciting because we can see from these instructions how to set the captives free.

Chapter 11 - Chosen Vessels

We are chosen of God to be His vessel a place where He can abide with us and we can abide with Him. Each person that God sent to the earth has an assignment from God and this is everyone born on the planet.

Since we are the earthen vessel that God uses to grow spiritual things, we must receive that spiritual seed from God and when we do and following the instructions to be vessels of honor, then God can honor us with His seed. God sent each of us here to accomplish the assignment that He had given us to do before we came to the planet. We all have a purpose for being here and when we know what that is and begin to do it we find that it is wonderful because we do that with excellence, it is not a chore or a burden and we can do it effortlessly. We wear that assignment like a suit tailor made for us, in fact when you do that you may not pay much attention to it but you do know that you get great satisfaction when you are doing that particular thing.

You may be thinking like I was that God could not possibly want me to do this or that because my history does not look like or sound like God at all but God knew what we would do when He sent us here and He is not going to change His mind just because we do not agree with Him. Nor does God look at what man looks at to determine if we deserve to work for Him or not. He already knows that we do not deserve or are not worthy of anything that is why He sent Jesus and it is trough Him that we are righteous before God.

If we have to look at some examples of this in the Bible to help us understand this the Apostle Paul is an examples of this, we can find the account of what happened when God made Him aware of his purpose for being on the earth in:

Act 9:13-15 Then Ananias answered, Lord, I have heard by many of this man, how much evil he hath done to thy saints at Jerusalem: ¹⁴ And here he hath authority from the chief priests to bind all that call on thy name. ¹⁵ But the Lord said unto him, Go thy way: for he is a <u>chosen vessel</u> unto me, to bear my name before the Gentiles, and kings, and the children of Israel KJV

Ananias had to ask God about Paul because it did seemed to him that Paul was against God and His people and maybe God did not realize that very important fact.

When we come to understand that we as believers function as earth and seed, we realize that sometimes we are the ground that people sow into and as that ground we grow things for them. At other times we are the seed that is sown into the ground of others. You can sow into my life and I can sow into your life, however we both have to realize that it is God that gives the increase and it is His power in the earth and in the seed. We had nothing to do with how God set that up. I believe that we misunderstand many spiritual things because we do not understand farming. God used farming to show us in the natural how this works in the spirit realm. God created the substance in the dirt of the earth to grow things and He created the substance in the seed that causes it to reproduce after its own kind. We get none of the credit for that but we can choose to allow God to use our vessel and make a decision that it will be a vessel of honor and not of dishonor.

Being a chosen vessel of God does not mean that we qualify in the natural realm of things because if it were up to society and social norms some of us would never get a chance to do anything because we have made too many bad decisions in our lives. While not all of our decisions were bad ones, the bad ones were enough to disqualify us for many things. Jesus did not see it that way. He does not check our credit report, He does not check our community standing, and He does not check our bank account or anything that we would consider making us worthy of His choosing us as His own. We did not choose ourselves unto God, He chose us and gives us opportunity to clean up our credit report, increase our bank account and be a beacon of light in our community.

Remember that John talks about Jesus choosing us in:

Jhn 15:16 Ye have not chosen me, but I have chosen you, and ordained you, that ye should go and bring forth fruit, and that your fruit should remain: that whatsoever ye shall ask of the Father in my name, he may give it you.

This is wonderful, because we do not have to sign up to unworthiness or condemnation. The Devil will try to take us there but we are chosen vessels we did not choose ourselves and God knew the condition of our vessels before the foundation of the world.

Jesus knew that the price that He would pay would be sufficient to present us faultless before God and therefore, He did not consider anything that our past presented as a problem. Jesus goes on to tell us because He has chosen us the world will hate us as it hates Him. He mentions that He has chosen us out of the world and therefore the world no longer loves us. The world will put many expectations on us to qualify for many things, but Jesus lets us know that we are not of the world and His expectations are different because we are already qualified and justified this is mentioned in:

Jhn 15:19 If ye were of the world, the world would love his own: but because ye are not of the world, but I have chosen you out of the world, therefore the world hateth you.

I wonder how many of us chosen vessels of God expect to be loved by the world, how many of us expect to be in good fellowship with those who are still in the world? If you are one that can say, yes that is me; I have good news for you. You are still chosen by God and He will bring you to His expected end, therefore, it does not matter that the world hates you because God loves you and He is your source for every aspect of your life.

We as the earth belong to God, He has placed His fullness in us and we are expected to use all of it. We find in:

Psa 24:1 - The earth is the LORD'S, and the fulness thereof; the world, and they that dwell therein. In this verse the word fullness in Hebrew is **mĕlo'** which means: that which fills, handful, multitude, that which fills, entire contents, full length, full line. While this passage is talking about the physical earth, we as earthen vessels enjoy the same fullness in the fullness of the Godhead. Paul talks about this in:

Col 2:6 As ye have therefore received Christ Jesus the Lord, so walk ye in him: and *Col 2:9-10 For in him dwelleth all the fulness of the Godhead bodily. 10 And ye are complete in him, which is the head of all principality and power:*

As children of God we have full access of all that Jesus Christ left for us. Having access to the fullness of the Godhead is something that most of us are not aware of and those that are aware do not consider some of it possible therefore we limit ourselves as to what we can do. Jesus said we would do greater works than He did. Jesus was only here three years, but we have many years to do what he did and there are so many more of us to do what He did. Jesus said this in:

Jhn 14:12 Verily, verily, I say unto you, He that believeth on me, the works that I do shall he do also; and greater works than these shall he do; because I go unto my Father.

What were some of the works that Jesus did? To name a few:

- Healed the sick
- Raised the dead
- Creative miracles of creating food for 5,000 with 2 fish and 5 loaves
- Set the captives free
- Changed water to wine
- Walked on water
- Became a living sacrifice
- Gentle as a lamb
- Strong as a lion
- Preached the gospel to the poor
- Healed the brokenhearted
- Preached deliverance to the captives
- Recovered sight to the blind
- Set at liberty them that were bruised and many more

If you understand fullness then all of this is in the package.

God has placed all of this in us and has given us an anointing to bring forth from Him through our earthen vessel all of the fullness of the Godhead. All we have to do is line our lives up with God's word concerning living a holy and righteous life and ask Jesus for whatever we need. Some people may understand what I am talking about but do not see any manifestation of the fullness happening in their lives. That is because God automatically expects us to live a holy life style. He knows that we can do that because

Jesus has freed us from the power and presence of sin and therefore we can refuse to let it have any place in our lives and God will back us up in this.

God wants us to be like Him in character and power, however, the character part sometimes challenges us because this is a process that happens over a period of time. We find this in:

Lev 20:7 Sanctify yourselves therefore, and be ye holy: for I am the LORD your God and in *1Pe 1:15-16 But as he which hath called you is holy, so be ye holy in all manner of conversation; Because it is written, Be ye holy; for I am holy.*

In Leviticus the word holy means to be set apart but then God said for them to sanctify themselves in order to be set apart. The Hebrew word for sanctify is **qadash** which means to consecrate, sanctify, prepare, dedicate, be hallowed, be holy, be sanctified, be separate. They had to purify themselves, however the Greek word holy in 1 Peter is **hagios** which means most holy thing, a saint.

This is what God has said that we are to be because that is what He is. This was explained by Paul to the Philippians in:

Phl 2:12-13 Wherefore, my beloved, as ye have always obeyed, not as in my presence only, but now much more in my absence, work out your own salvation with fear and trembling. 13 For it is God which worketh in you both to will and to do of his good pleasure.

God wants us to be free of any hold that Satan has on us and He wants to help us do it by getting rid of the habitual sin that we may have and by making sure that we have nothing in us that Satan can attach himself to or touch. The Greek word for work out in this passage is **katergazomai** which means to perform, accomplish, achieve, to work out i.e. to do that from which something results, of things: bring about, result in, to fashion i.e. render one fit for a thing.

Now, we can see from this that God wants us to grow up in Him and get rid of the things that are not like Him. This however, is a process; it is not accomplished immediately when we are first saved. God does not ask us to get rid of the sin that we fellowship with when we come to Him, He knows that we need help to get that accomplished, He wants us to come just the way we are but He does not want us to stay that way. He wants us to be free of the chains, bondages or strongholds etc. that Satan has us trapped in and once we are free He wants us to use the fullness of His power to go forth and get someone else free.

I cannot tell you how much I thank God for the people that He sent to me to help me in different stages of my life to get up and get out of some of my challenges. I knew that I needed to be free; I knew that I needed to stop doing certain things because they were not of God the results and consequence at the end of that thing was not going to be good. I could not do it by myself, I knew that I needed help, there were many people that wanted to help but they did not have the authority or power from God to use that portion of their fullness, but thanks be to God there were some people He specifically sent to me that did have the authority and power from God to help me and they did and I am free of those things.

I have heard people say that when they get to heaven that they will not have to put up with any of the bad things that plague us in this life here on earth, but they did not realize that God wants us saved from the snare of the Devil here on earth, God wants us saved from the tricks, the deception and lies of the Devil. These are things that we can be saved from right now; we do not have to wait until we get to heaven. However, we have to start by getting rid of the sin that our flesh has gotten use to all of these years because participating in the things of the Devil did not feel bad to our flesh, our flesh will fight us to keep them. We can fast and pray to help us get rid of some things. But we may need help to get rid of some other things.

God wants you and me to be to be free and to help others. He wants us to use our vessels to bring forth His fullness for success in our personal lives, to help others and to do it all for His glory because that is His will for us all. The end result of any sin is death. It does not matter what we think about our particular issue, if it is sin the end result is death in that thing. That is the reason God does not want us to participate in sin. He wants us to be victorious in every aspect of our lives, not just a few areas.

I know that people have said that they got away with doing this sin or the other sin, but that was because they did not recognized the harvest of the crop that the sin seed produced, its crop of death. They usually blame it on someone else, some organization, the government entity or anything but themselves and that was because they were blinded by the Devil. That is not the case for everybody but sometimes we miss the mark and we can't get out because we have been blinded and tricked.

For instance, have you ever known people who repeat bad cycles once or twice a year? They recognized the cycle but they blame someone or something else for doing it, not the Devil. I will use this example to give better understanding: if there is a person that cannot keep a job longer than a year and find themselves constantly looking for employment indicates a problem somewhere with this situation.

After about 5 years and 20 jobs they are still complaining about the bad and terrible boss they had or how miserable the company treats employees or how horrible people are treated in that particular place of employment. If they do not recognized that the only common factor in all 20 of these jobs or places of employment was them, they will never find out what it is in them that is causing them to lose employment or to be fired.

They will stay in this cycle forever and never be able to keep employment for more than a short period of time. They may struggle with a quick temper, they may lack the ability to follow directions or maybe they do not like to submit to authority. It could be anything, but they will never know if they do not get help from someone that is willing to tell them the truth with and by the leading of Holy Spirit. None of these employers know each other and the purpose of taking employment is to get the money they offer, therefore it is important to know how to maintain employment without continuing to complaints of being done wrong by all of these different people. It is a trick of the Devil to keep people in bondage and to keep them blind to their own sin that the Devil is using to keep them bound and defeated.

God does not want our vessels plagued with defeat. But it is impossible to live victoriously in a lifestyle of habitual sin situations. Therefore, as we become more and more like Him we begin to discover that the mystery of our earthen vessels is found in the authority and power that comes with the fullness of the Godhead.

Now we can take another look at this verse in:

Psa 24:1 - The earth is the LORD'S, and the fulness thereof; the world, and they that dwell therein.

We see from this verse that everything belongs to God and since it all belongs to God He has the right to do with it as He pleases, yet He allows us to choose. The earth that is the soil on and in the ground and the earth that is the vessel we live in that is also the temple where the Holy Spirit resides within us.

It is amazing to me every time I think about how wonderfully and beautifully we are made in His image after His likeness as seen in:

Gen 1:26 And God said, Let us make man in our image, after our likeness: and let them have dominion over the fish of the sea, and over the fowl of the air, and over the cattle, and over all the earth, and over every creeping thing that creepeth upon the earth.

This indicates that we are made in the image and after the likeness of the Godhead:

> Not just the Father, who's assignment is to create and destroy
> Not just the Son (Christ) who's assignment is to save and redeem
> Not just the Holy Spirit who's assignment is to sustain the saved and redeemed

But as all three of them, we have the fullness of the Godhead.

After God did that then He said let them have dominion over the fowl, of the air, over the cattle, over all of the earth and every creeping thing that creeps upon the earth. Now take a look at this great assignment, how is man going to do that? He will do it by using what God gave him to use.

God expects us to operate as He does and if we understand what it means to operate as He does we can also understand what His likeness does and we can do what He left for us to do using all the means that He has given us to do it. Since the earth is His and all the fullness thereof that means that we are made to house the fullness of God in our earthen vessel. Our vessel is a natural physical body, however, nothing about the fullness of God is physical, it is all spiritual but it is difficult to understand spiritual things without a natural physical example and that is why God gives us the natural physical examples to help us understand the spiritual things.

If we understand how to grow things in the natural we can better understand how to grow things in the spirit realm. We know if we plant corn in the natural we are going to get a harvest of corn, we also know that we must have corn seeds to plant corn and thus we understand planting seeds in the spiritual realm will harvest us a crop of that seed in the spiritual realm. It is hard for some to imagine God's plan for their lives because they do not understand that when God gives us an assignment or a Word concerning His plan for your life, He fully intends to prepare you to receive it if you do not already have that working in your life.

I remember, the other day I was asking God for something and I did not consider any of the things that I had already asked Him for. I should have because I realize that many of them have not manifested in my life yet. I know that I received it when I prayed because His word says that we have what we ask for at the point of prayer, if we ask according to His word. When I ask this time Holy Spirit said to me, I have given you everything that you asked me for, but I must prepare you to receive it. Every time you ask for something new you must start the process of preparation to receive what you asked for.

That caused me to think, because at that point I had not considered that I may have already started two or three processes to become what I had asked God for. That meant that I must be dying in some areas and that I needed to kill the crop of seed that I had planted that were not of God. Things that were dear to my heart that I needed to get rid of or things that I needed to plant seeds for to add to my life.

When Holy Spirit said that all I could say is WOW! I cannot imagine how many preparation processes that I had started and never finished because I was not aware of the process of becoming what I had asked, therefore when the pressure became great I abandon the process and started something else. The reality of that is that I will have to start all over again to finish all of the processes that I abandoned.

I thought that when I asked God for something if I did not get it in a certain period of time the answer was no or not now. It never occurred to me that I had to finish a process in order to receive a particular thing. God said His answer was yes to all that I asked but I was not prepared to receive at the time that I asked. I also realize that I have asked for things that God was never going to give me because they were not of Him. I did not know it at the time but those things have to come from the devil because of the nature of the request. I had asked for them out of my anger or my hurt and God will never violate His word no matter what is going on with us as individuals or groups.

God gives instruction and direction in His word of how to respond to anger or hurt and that is what He expects us to do. We can never go to God our Father with a complaint about one of our siblings and expect Him to let us spank them. We are all His children and He is a good Father, He knows how to handle all of us. That is completely out of God's order. He is not going to change His order just because we have issues or difficulties. We are the ones that have to conform to His word; He is not going to change His word to fit our situation. We must change our situation by using His word and letting it grow in and flow to and through this earthen vessel that He has given us. This means that we have to begin to plant what we want to grow in the next harvest season. Whatever our situation is God wants us to be able to change it if it needs changing.

God has created a fail proof system for us and if we obey His word and follow His direction we will win every time. God has eliminated the almost and the maybes. It is us that keep these two alive. When we understand what happens in the natural when we plant things then we know what to expect when we plant things in the spiritual realm. If we plant a seed of love then the harvest is that of love. The harvest may not come immediately because the natural process of seedtime and harvest is seasonal, but we know that God is the Lord over the harvest. Part of our responsibility as believers is to reach the world and spread the gospel of Jesus Christ and there is a harvest that God is looking for as lord of the harvest and that is found in:

Mat 9:38 Pray ye therefore the Lord of the harvest, that he will send forth labourers into his harvest.

This passage is talking about the harvest of souls; there are people that God wants us to speak to. There are people waiting on us to bring them the good news of the gospel and there are people with no shepherd and they are looking for the Lord. Our harvest is not just of things, we plant seeds in the lives of people that will eventually bring them to Christ.

God can have one season overtake another. We know that it takes rain to grow things in the natural; the word of God talks specifically about the former and the latter rain and each comes in its own season and its own month.

Deu 11:14 That I will give you the rain of your land in his due season, the first rain and the latter rain, that thou mayest gather in thy corn, and thy wine, and thine oil,

This of course indicates a process of time and is the normal process of how things are grown in their normal season, however, on occasion God does override the season, the time, the normal process of the rain and the harvest. We see that in:

Joel 2:23 Be glad then, ye children of Zion, and rejoice in the LORD your God: for he hath given you the former rain moderately, and he will cause to come down for you the rain, the former rain, and the latter rain in the first month, and also in *Amos 9:13 Behold, the days come, saith the LORD, that the plowman shall overtake the reaper, and the treader of grapes him that soweth seed; and the mountains shall drop sweet wine, and all the hills shall melt.*

Either way, you win, whether it is over a process of time or whether it happens instantly God is in control. You have the ability to change your situation or someone else's by planting and growing the word of God in your chosen vessel, the temple of the only true and living God.

The power that God has given the earth is truly amazing to me. The earth's ability to grow things is taken for granted most of the time. Most of the people that I know or have known who have planted things into the earth never considered that the earth would not grow it. They never considered how the earth did what it needed to do to grow things nor did they consider that the earth would refuse their offering of seed. All of this is because of God's original design of the earth to bring forth a plant or a tree from whatever seed that was planted in it. How do we accomplish this as an earthen chosen vessel? We plant the word of God in our vessel and allow it to bring forth the manifestation of God's word.

About the Author
Dr. Cynthia V. White

Cynthia V. White graduated from Ballard Hudson High School in Macon, Georgia. She continued her education at Morris Brown College, Atlanta, Georgia where she received a Bachelor of Science Degree in Mathematics and Education. Cynthia has also received a Master of Arts in Biblical Studies, Master of Divinity and a Doctor of Ministry from Maple Springs Baptist Bible College and Seminary, Capitol Heights, Maryland.

Cynthia was employed by the Department of the Navy for 31 years. During her tenure there she was the head of the following departments: Computer Aided Design and Manufacturing, Industrial Improvement Technologies, Joint Electronic Drawings and Manufacturing of Industrial Data, Military Construction Projects, Service Craft Management, and Manufacturing Technology Program Manager for Naval Shipyards. Cynthia is an accomplished conference speaker. She has spoken at the national productivity conferences, naval engineering conferences, research conferences, production conferences, and general business conferences.

Cynthia is a strong supporter of community services. She has participated in fund raisers for the March of Dimes, she supports children in need programs, she is a past Chairman of the Board of Directors of the Center for

Community Development of Housing for the Mentally Ill and the Aged. She is also a past member of the Board of Directors of Bethel House, a community support center for people in need of help and assistance of food, housing, education, jobs, and other needs.

Cynthia is currently a member of Heritage Church International, Waldorf, Maryland where Bishop Rodney S. Walker I. serves as senior pastor. Under Bishop Walker's leadership and covering Cynthia serves as the Secretary of Records of the church, Office Manager and she also served as past manager of Kingdom Christian Book. She serves on the staff of Heritage Church International as Chief Elder, the Overseer of the apostolic arm of the ministry and as an Associate Pastor. She has ministered as a conference speaker for women, prophetic conferences, financial and business conferences and workshops. She has taught Bible Study at the Department of the Navy under the direction of the Chaplain for the Naval Sea System Command.

Cynthia serves in Bishop R. S. Walker Ministries, where Bishop R. S. Walker is founder and President, as registrar and head of the registration department of the School of the Prophets. She also serves as a Prophetic Presbyter of the Ministry.

Cynthia is the owner and the CEO of her own business. She is an accomplished author. She has published seven books, Understanding Spiritual Maturity, The Christian Torah, What Your Father Never Told You about Business,

The Importance of Seed, Winning Battles With Love, and The Sycamore Fig Tree – A Living Sacrifice and the Power of the Earth. She has spoken at several conferences on the subjects of the books.

www.ingramcontent.com/pod-product-compliance
Lightning Source LLC
Chambersburg PA
CBHW071147090426
42736CB00012B/2266